The Woman

The volume includes a group of poems, stories and essays written for *The Woman*. Some were published in the programme for the first production. Some appear here for the first time.

The photograph on the front of the cover shows Yvonne Bryceland in the production of The Woman *at the Olivier Theatre. Both this and the photograph of Edward Bond on the back of the cover are reproduced by courtesy of Chris Davies.*

Edward Bond

THE WOMAN

Scenes of War and Freedom

A Mermaid Dramabook
HILL AND WANG   New York
A division of Farrar, Straus and Giroux

© *1979 by Edward Bond*
Printed in Great Britain

ISBN 0–8090–9782–6
ISBN 0–8090–1241–3 *paperback*

For Peggy

CAST

The Greeks

ISMENE
HEROS
NESTOR
THERSITES
AJAX
HIGH PRIEST
SECOND PRIEST
CHAPLAIN
CAPTAIN
AIDE
CHIEF ARCHITECT
MAID
CALLIS ⎫
LAKIS ⎬ Soldiers
ARTOS ⎪
CRIOS ⎭
TWO DRUNK SOLDIERS
SAILOR
OTHER SOLDIERS AND OFFICERS

The Trojans

HECUBA
CASSANDRA
SON
ASTYANAX
HIGH PRIEST
SECOND PRIEST
CHAPLAIN
AIDE
THREE WOMEN WITH PLAGUE
MIDDLE CLASS BYSTANDERS

TWO ATTENDANTS TO HECUBA
SOLDIERS
THE POOR

Villagers

PORPOISE, a woman
TEMI, her husband
ROSSA ⎤
DEMA ⎬ Young girls
GEMIL ⎦
KALERA ⎤
NIMPUS ⎬ Women
FALGAR ⎦
ORVO ⎤
HYSPOS ⎬ Young men
DARIO ⎦
OTHER VILLAGERS

THE DARK MAN

Note: Many of the parts can be doubled. The Dark Man must not be doubled. The first production had a cast of forty-three.

LIST OF SCENES

PART ONE
One : Greek HQ
Two : Greek Commander's Quarters
Three : Greek Look-out post
Four : Troy – palace
Five : Greek HQ
Six : Troy – palace
Seven : Troy – prison
Eight : Greek HQ
Nine : Battle ground

The Woman was first performed by the National Theatre Company at the Olivier Theatre, London. The production opened on 10th August 1978 with the following cast:

The Greeks

HEROS	Nicky Henson
ISMENE	Susan Fleetwood
NESTOR	Andrew Cruickshank
THERSITES	James Grant
AJAX	Gawn Grainger
HIGH PRIEST	Brian Kent
CHAPLAIN	Norman Claridge
DEACON	Peter Jolley
CAPTAIN	Peter Needham
AIDE	Ray Edwards
CHIEF ARCHITECT	Brian Kent
MAID	Irene Gorst
CALLIS	Derek Thompson
LAKIS SOLDIERS	Michael Beint
ARTOS	Glyn Grain
CRIOS	Harry Meacher
TWO DRUNK SOLDIERS	Chris Hallam
	Keith Skinner
SAILOR	Richard Perkins

OTHER SOLDIERS AND OFFICERS
Alexander Allenby, Elliot Cooper, Roger Gartland, Peter Jolley, Adam Norton, Richard Perkins

The Trojans

HECUBA	Yvonne Bryceland
SON	Dermot Crowley
CASSANDRA	Dinah Stabb
ASTYANAX	Timothy Norton or
	Grant Warnock

HIGH PRIEST	Anthony Douse
CHAPLAIN	Stanley Lloyd
DEACON	Alexander Allenby
AIDE	Harry Meacher
THREE WOMEN WITH PLAGUE	Margaret Ford
	Marianne Morley
	Tel Stevens

BYSTANDERS

Norman Claridge, Irene Gorst, Anna Manahan,
Peggy Marshall, Harry Meacher

HECUBA'S ATTENDANTS	Brenda Dowsett
	Jane Evers

SOLDIERS

Elliot Cooper, Ray Edwards, Adam Norton,
Richard Perkins, David Pugh, Keith Skinner

THE POOR

Alexander Allenby, Michael Beint, Sheraton Blount,
Anthony Douse, Brenda Dowsett, Jane Evers,
Margaret Ford, Roger Gartland, Glyn Grain,
Chris Hallam, Peter Jolley, Brian Kent, Louisa
Livingstone, Stanley Lloyd, Marianne Morley, Peter
Needham, Tel Stevens, Derek Thompson

The Villagers

PORPOISE	Anna Manahan
TEMI	Anthony Douse
PATRIARCH	Norman Claridge
MIDWIFE	Marianne Morley
KALERA	Peggy Marshall
HYSPOS'S GRANDFATHER	Stanley Lloyd
HYSPOS'S FATHER	Peter Needham
HYSPOS'S MOTHER	Brenda Dowsett
COXSWAINS	Michael Beint
	Gawn Grainger
	James Grant

CARPENTER	David Pugh
PREGNANT LADY	Tel Stevens
NIMPUS	Irene Gorst
FALGAR	Jane Evers
HYSPOS	Derek Thompson
DARIO	Dermot Crowley
ORVO	Roger Gartland
ALIOS	Keith Skinner
TYROS	Adam Norton
MANOS	Glyn Grain
ROSSA	Margaret Ford
DEMA	Louisa Livingstone
GEMIL	Sheraton Blount
LAPU	Elliot Cooper
THE DARK MAN	Paul Freeman

Directed by Edward Bond
Designed by Hayden Griffin
Costumes by Hayden Griffin and Stephen Skaptason
Lighting by Andy Phillips
Music for the songs by Hans Werner Henze

Part One

ONE

Greek camp. Headquarters.
NESTOR *asleep on a stool.*

SOLDIERS (*off*). Dead. Dead.
THERSITES (*off*). Priam dead!

    A moment later THERSITES *runs on shouting.*

  Hurrah! (*To* NESTOR.) Priam dead!
SOLDIERS (*off*). Dead. Hurrah.
THERSITES (*running out*). Priam dead!

    THERSITES *runs off.*

SOLDIERS (*off*). Priam dead.

    AJAX *runs on.*

AJAX (*to* NESTOR). Priam's dead!

    AJAX *runs off.*

SOLDIERS (*off*). Dead. Dead.
NESTOR (*waking*). What?
SOLDIERS (*off*). Hurrah.

    THERSITES *and* AJAX *run back. They embrace. Off, cheers and cries of* 'Dead' *are heard throughout the scene.*

THERSITES. The bastard's dead!
AJAX. Rotting!
NESTOR. Who is?
THERSITES. Priam!
SOLDIERS (*off*). Dead. Dead. Dead.

NESTOR. Dead?

AJAX. Yes yes yes!

HEROS *comes on.*

THERSITES (to HEROS). That's why the city was quiet. He's been dying for weeks.

NESTOR. Priam's dead?

AJAX. The fight'll go out of them now!

THERSITES. Give them a month!

AJAX. They'll all be dead.

NESTOR (*embracing* AJAX *and* THERSITES). My boys! I shall see Greece again!

HEROS. We must hold a council. If we miss this chance we could be here for years.

NESTOR. Stools! Stools!

An ORDERLY *brings on the officers' stools.*

HEROS. Do we know what he died of?

AJAX. Old age!

NESTOR. Not killed?

THERSITES. Some children came up on the wall playing funerals. We shouted up and they said: the king's dead. Then their guards came back and called them down from inside.

NESTOR. I'm sorry he wasn't killed.

AJAX. We heard priests chanting.

HEROS. Let's sit.

They sit.

AJAX. Hecuba will run Troy now. He chose Hecuba – not his son.

HEROS. We've sat outside Troy for five years. This is our first chance.

NESTOR. I'm surprised he lasted so long. He was old when he married Hecuba. Older than I am now. (*Laughter.*) It's true – long thin man with a white beard and little piggy eyes. Even on a calm day he looked doubled up in the wind.

HEROS. He'd have compromised in the end – Hecuba won't.

THERSITES. Her son might make her.

HEROS. When her husband couldn't?

AJAX. You think they'll –

ISMENE *comes in.*

ISMENE. Is Priam dead?

HEROS. Yes thank God!

NESTOR. No women in council. Bad luck.

THERSITES. Ismene might be able to advise us.

NESTOR. Advise us?

THERSITES. Now Troy's run by a woman.

NESTOR. Well . . .

HEROS. Let Ismene stay. What Thersites says is true.

THERSITES *gives his stool to* ISMENE.

Well.

AJAX. You think they'll fight on?

THERSITES. Won't they just –

HEROS. Let's review the situation. Twenty-five years ago Troy
was already a falling city and Athens in the ascent. My father'd
won his war for the Eastern mines. He'd captured the statue of
the Goddess of Good Fortune and was bringing it to Athens.
Hecuba told Priam that if he owned the statue Troy would be
saved. He took it – and since then Troy's had nothing but
disasters. Why? The statue brings good fortune only to those
destined to own her. But how can we win the war and capture
the statue of Good Fortune when we haven't got the statue to
give us the good fortune to win the war?

AJAX. That's the problem.

HEROS. Well, no man's hand can be more impious than the
Trojans': to hold what all men call the supreme goddess against
her will! On such men the greatest misfortune must fall. What
is their greatest misfortune? That we should win the war. This
proves that we must.

NESTOR. In a nutshell.

HEROS. But for that very reason Troy must fight. They fight but can't win – the goddess of Good Fortune will punish them by giving us the victory. I know what's happening in Troy. It's so clear in my head. Listen! – I'll tell you.

A scene inside Troy

PRIAM on a bier. HECUBA, CASSANDRA *and the* SON. HECUBA *wears ceremonial mourning. She is made up like an old aristocratic whore. She looks tragic but doesn't cry.* CASSANDRA *has a round face, long fair hair, and is pale and has been crying. The* SON *is a little short and thickset, but he moves simply and is dressed heroically. The scene has an air of theatricality.*

Note : in the first production HECUBA *was played by* NESTOR, CASSANDRA *by* THERSITES *and the* SON *by* AJAX. PRIAM'*s body was invisible. There were no* PRIESTS. *The scene is to be imagined as occurring in* HEROS'*s head.*

HECUBA. Burn Priam before the war temple and scatter his ashes – (*She turns to the* SON.) – on the battlefield yourself.

SON. Mother! Even my father's funeral – she uses that to put my life in danger.

CASSANDRA. Yes, mother – that's dangerous!

SON. It's only done for heroes who died in battle.

HECUBA. If he was your age he'd have gone on the battlefield and sent the Greeks packing – we'd have celebrated victory long ago!

SON. If you'd let him he'd have given the Greeks everything at the start – lock stock and barrel!

HECUBA. Cover his ears! They say the dead still hear voices from this world for a time. He lies there and can't strike his son while he insults his mother!

SON. You bully people by acting! She treats this city as if it was on a stage.

CASSANDRA (*wearily*). Please.

SON. You worry what he hears when he's dead! She shouted at him every day when he was alive!

HECUBA (*turns away and talks almost to herself*). Who will help me? What can I lean on? – not even this wall. My enemies sit out there and wait for it to crumble. If it was iron they'd wait for it to rust. They have the patience of the damned. I'm shut up with the spiders that will build webs on my tomb.

CASSANDRA. Mother.

HECUBA. No, I won't be comforted. (*She takes the ring from Priam's finger and holds it over her head between finger and thumb.*) Your father made me head of the city. He swore an oath in the temple. Who speaks against his oath? (*No answer. She ceremoniously puts her finger into the ring.*) People, war, armies, cities! I would like to sit at home and hear myself say children, friends, family – the words of my girlhood. If you were a leader, a soldier, I'd be on my knees begging: mercy, don't take such risks, don't go to the wall today. Instead you make me shout like an old hag – and blame me for it! (*Turns away from him.*) When I'm dead the Greeks can come over that wall and cut this city open. Then let them kill and burn and loot! I'll give them nothing.

The SON *goes.* PRIESTS *follow with the bier.*

A sullen child who obeys out of fear. He'll throw his father's ashes as if he was throwing them in my teeth! He understands nothing. At least there should be peace in our homes. Instead – (*She doesn't finish the sentence.*) There! The same words: hate, fear, war, prison.

CASSANDRA. Give the statue to the Greeks. Without father to guide us –

HECUBA. Trust the Greeks? No, I'll never do that. What would the Greeks have to lose once they'd got it? We must hold on to it – that's the only way to save our lives.

HECUBA *and* CASSANDRA *follow the* PRIESTS *out.*

ISMENE. But why d'you say she –

NESTOR. No woman-talk in council! Well now: how long will the
war last? Till it ends. When will it end? Hecuba's old – but the
Trojans are long-livers. Take Priam!

HEROS. Nestor, go home. You've served Greece long enough.
Spend your last years in that nice house by the sea.

NESTOR. I'm not an old dodderer yet! What would my soldiers do
if I left? They love their old Nestor.

THERSITES. Send a delegation to Hecuba. Offer to go if she gives
us the statue. No plunder, burning, forced labour.

AJAX. After five years? Listen to your men: When we get through
those gates – women, loot, drink, arson!

NESTOR. At my age you don't live long enough to enjoy revenge
when you've got it. The wine's better on my own hill, and I'm
useless to women. But the men want to go home with some
silver in their pockets, a piece of material for the wife, and a
Trojan helmet to put on and frighten the kiddies.

THERSITES. Tell them they can leave tomorrow – or wait years for
a piece of material. They'll get good wages in Athens – building
the new city will pay well. Or they could have land –

AJAX. You'll hand over your estates?

THERSITES. In the colonies.

AJAX. That would mean more fighting.

THERSITES. At least it'd be a new war with different scenery.

ISMENE. I think the men would rather –

HEROS. Ismene –

ISMENE. It's obvious! Look how they try to turn their quarters
into homes, as if their wives were looking after them! Some of
them married girls from the countryside here – they want to
take them home to their parents.

HEROS. If we promise the Trojans something we must keep our
word. Remember, the goddess sees and judges. It's difficult to
control men in the last days of a war. Do we want to leave Troy
killing our own men when the Trojans couldn't? Is that what
the goddess wants?

NESTOR. We'd have to guarantee – in the eyes of the goddess – to try to restrain them. No one could do more than that.

HEROS. Let's vote.

NESTOR *and* THERSITES *put up their hands.*

AJAX. I'm against! The enemy's lost its leader –

ISMENE. He says the leader was always Hecuba.

AJAX. – so let's wait and see how this affects their morale. This vote can change the whole course of the war. How does our commander vote?

HEROS. There's a lot to be said on both sides. I'm for sending a delegation – on balance.

THERSITES. Three one.

ISMENE. Hecuba will be more likely to listen if your delegation has a woman.

NESTOR. That's too much!

THERSITES. The situation's new. We must adapt to it. I'll go with Ismene and do the talking.

NESTOR. Then go! It's usual to send the oldest – and therefore wisest – member of the council. I give up my place to Thersites!

NESTOR *goes out.*

HEROS. So, Thersites and my wife? (AJAX *and* THERSITES *nod.* HEROS *beckons to* AJAX.) You.

HEROS *and* AJAX *go.*

THERSITES. Why did your husband vote for the compromise? He must destroy Troy – his power in Athens depends on it.

ISMENE. Wishes don't change but the cost of fulfilling them changes all the time. When Miron wanted to make the sculpture of a discus thrower the only man who could hold the pose long enough was a cripple who couldn't move. You fight beside him – what do you think?

THERSITES. You know him better than I do.

TWO

Greek camp – HEROS'*s quarters.*
Night. HEROS *stands before an open window looking across at Troy.*
A MAID *is folding back the bed sheets for the night.* ISMENE *comes in.*
She wears a nightgown.

MAID. Good night sir.
HEROS. Thank you.
MAID. Ma'am.
ISMENE. Good night.

    The MAID *goes.*

ISMENE. You're not angry?
HEROS (*looking round at her*). At what?
ISMENE. Me going to Troy?
HEROS (*turning back*). No.
ISMENE. I wonder what she'll look like.
HEROS. You won't see for paint. (*He goes on looking out.*) Her husband married her when he was old. That's the most ruttish sort of infatuation. My father met her. He understood Priam. All that old man's excesses lie at her door. She pushed him.
ISMENE. I meant the statue.
HEROS. Ah. When I was a child people still called Troy the fabulous city of the East. We played sacking Troy. Now I stand in front of it and it's a closed coffin with someone moving inside.
ISMENE. Will you keep your word? No killing or looting?
HEROS. Athens will want me to pay for the war. Cheap labour would have helped. (*He goes to the desk and prepares to write.*) Who shall *I* trust? God? Ask the soldiers! The government? (*He looks across to the window.*) It's a beautiful night. If I make mistakes I'm punished – by the government or the troops or God. I'm God to my men – obviously I am. Does God cheat? I don't know. (*He starts to write.*) I must tell Athens Priam's dead.

ISMENE *gets into bed.*

(*Writing.*) I was born at a time when I summed up a nation's strength. My father had doubts, my heirs will have weaknesses. Of course I'm only a dummy on Athens's knees: but the voice is clear in me. They say the ewe killed in the compound to celebrate my birth had human milk in the udder. (*He looks up towards the window.*) The stars are very clear tonight. (*He looks down at his hand.*) My fingers look like five white towers. (*He puts down the pen and looks across at* ISMENE.) The death of a king requires a certain prolixity. (*Slight pause.*) When circumstances change, strengths become weaknesses. Let's get home to Athens and build it quickly! – so we're still young when we lead the first kid to the altar. (*Slight pause. He stands.*) I'm going round the lines.

HEROS *goes out.*

THREE

Greek look-out.
Morning. Three private soldiers. LAKIS *stands on duty.* CALLIS *and* ARTOS *lounge on the ground. All three are quiet, relaxed, but watchful. They are armed with long spear poles, narrowed to a simple point at the end.*

CALLIS. Take a good look. You'll miss it when we're gone. (LAKIS *kicks a stone at* CALLIS.) Don't worry, you'll be here longer than that will. You'll be kicking up its dust when you're marching.

LAKIS. Up you get.

CALLIS (*not moving*). Why d'you want to go home anyway? Your old mother thinks she's rid of you. She'll have a nasty turn when she finds you on the doorstep. Then you say: Take my nice little Trojan wife to the kitchen. O, she'll be very pleased.

ARTOS. You taking her back?

LAKIS. Yes.

ARTOS. Will she go?

LAKIS. Yes.

ARTOS. When I ask mine she just laughs. You can't really tell with a Trojan. Her family's shut up in there and I'm out here shovelling earth on top of them. One day she might spit in my face.

LAKIS. You treat her all right.

CALLIS. Sometimes.

ARTOS. I've gone in unexpected and found her crying.

CALLIS. Hey!

LAKIS. What?

CALLIS. Is it still there?

LAKIS. Find out!

> LAKIS *jerks* CALLIS *to his feet.* CALLIS *takes* LAKIS's *place on watch. He picks up a spear.*

ARTOS. Mine!

CALLIS. Sorry. (*He picks up his own spear. Looks at Troy.*) O, it's moved. To the right. I tell a lie – the left. (*The others laugh briefly.*) Like staring at the back of a mirror for five years. You end up forgetting what you look like.

ARTOS. No loss in your case.

CALLIS. That wall's marked you for life. You're its! Even if you got home your girl'd be homesick for that wall. When we're daft old buggers we'll talk about it for hours – as if this was the good time. Hey!

> LAKIS *and* CALLIS *stand and stare off stage.*

LAKIS. What?

CALLIS. Two!

LAKIS. Running?

CALLIS (*suddenly*). There! Three!

ARTOS. What on earth . . .? Women!

CALLIS (*through his teeth*). Weird.

LAKIS (*to* CALLIS). Get the captain.

ARTOS. *Wait . . .* ! Women! – we stand to do ourselves all right.

LAKIS. But –

CALLIS. They're running!

ARTOS. Refugees! We're onto a good thing.

CALLIS. What if they're armed?

ARTOS. Women running towards us with open arms and legs!

CALLIS. It's a dream!

> *The men watch tensely in silence. Three* VEILED WOMEN *run on. They stop for a moment and glance at each other. Then they mince towards the* SOLDIERS *with open arms.*

ARTOS. Giving yourselves up!

LAKIS. Wait!

ARTOS. Hello lovely!

> *The* FIRST WOMAN *reaches* CALLIS. *She embraces him wildly, panting.* ARTOS *panics and dodges away from the* SECOND WOMAN.

CALLIS. Let's see what you've got for a – (*He pulls the veil off. Her face is deformed.*) Agh!

> *The* FIRST WOMAN *clings to* CALLIS. *He screams and tries to beat and kick her off.* LAKIS *kills her with his spear. The* SECOND *and* THIRD WOMEN *are chasing* ARTOS.

LAKIS. Plague!

CALLIS. Agh! I touched her!

ARTOS. Plague!

> LAKIS *turns on the* SECOND *and* THIRD WOMEN *with his spear. They run out.*

LAKIS (*to* ARTOS). The captain!

> ARTOS *runs out.* CALLIS *writhes on the ground to clean himself.*

CALLIS. She spat at me! Here!
LAKIS. Wash! You must wash!
CALLIS. Filth!

> CALLIS *staggers towards* LAKIS. LAKIS *backs, keeping him off with his spear.*

LAKIS. Wash!

> CALLIS *runs out. The* SECOND WOMAN *creeps quickly on behind* LAKIS. *He takes a few steps towards the body of the* FIRST WOMAN *and peers down at her.*

LAKIS. God. Skin like a slug.

> *The* SECOND WOMAN *jumps on* LAKIS's *back. She clings and bites. He struggles, throws her off and spears her. She falls down.* LAKIS *runs out after* CALLIS. *The* SECOND WOMAN *gets to her knees, stretches out her hands towards Troy and creeps a few paces towards it.*

SECOND WOMAN. . . . Troy . . .

> ARTOS *comes on with the* CAPTAIN *and other* SOLDIERS. *They watch the* SECOND WOMAN *a moment as she stretches out her hands and creeps towards Troy. She is too wounded to notice them. The* CAPTAIN *kills her.*

CAPTAIN. Fanatics! Where's the others?
ARTOS. The river! They touched them!
CAPTAIN (*to* FIRST SOLDIER). Keep watch!

> FIRST SOLDIER *takes up sentry post.*

They touched you?
ARTOS. O no.
FIRST SOLDIER (*pointing off*). There's one! And there – another one!
CAPTAIN and SOLDIERS (*shouting a warning*). Plague! Plague! Watch your front!

CAPTAIN. They won't get through. A general alert.

FIRST SOLDIER (*looking at the dead* WOMEN). God what a sight!

CAPTAIN. Stay at your post! (*To* ARTOS.) They got them drunk then pushed them out.

> AJAX *comes on with an* AIDE. *He goes straight to the dead bodies and looks.*

AJAX (*to* AIDE). All berserkers killed on sight. Dogs, rats, birds and so on. All lines kept lit at night.

AIDE. Sir.

> AIDE *goes out.* FIRST SOLDIER *reacts as he watches other* WOMEN *being chased off stage.*

CAPTAIN. More coming across, sir – (*Gestures off stage.*) – but the men know.

AJAX (*to* ARTOS). You were here?

ARTOS. Sir –

AJAX. How did they get so close? Court martial, Captain.

CAPTAIN (*to* SECOND SOLDIER). You.

> SECOND SOLDIER *takes charge of* ARTOS.

FIRST SOLDIER (*looking off*). They got one sir! Go on, go on!

AJAX (*to* CAPTAIN, *indicating the bodies*). Get rid of them.

CAPTAIN. Sir.

> THERSITES *comes on.*

AJAX (*looks towards the city*). Look – they're burning the bodies!

> *They all stare silently towards the city.*

THERSITES. A pall of black smoke is being slowly lowered over the city as if it was a coffin – and they go on fighting!

> HEROS *comes on.*

ARTOS (*to* SECOND SOLDIER). That'll stink . . . Great oily black smuts in your hair and clothes and food . . .

AJAX. Carry on.

> ARTOS *and* SECOND SOLDIER *go out. The* CAPTAIN *posts another sentry and goes out with the rest of the* SOLDIERS. *The* OFFICERS *look towards the city.*

AJAX. I'll move the men back to the ships.

HEROS. Not necessary.

AJAX. Put a cordon between them and the city.

HEROS. That smoke might be a trick. We can't withdraw and leave their way open to the countryside –

THERSITES. But in a plague we always –

HEROS. No. Pay the men a bonus. Gentlemen, if and when we are infected, *then* we'll consider withdrawing.

AJAX. But plague! – they'll feed their dogs on bodies and chase them out to our lines –

HEROS. Surely you see? One loophole – and they'll take the statue out of the city and hide it in the mountains. We'd never find it.

THERSITES (*shrugs*). They probably smuggled it out long ago.

HEROS. No, not till they're desperate. The plague may make them desperate. This is the very worst time to pull back.

THERSITES. Yes – but if we lose our whole army –

HEROS. You speak as if the plague was punishing us! Troy has the plague! Can't you see? – the goddess has taken us one more step closer to victory!

> *They go.*

FOUR

Troy – the palace.
HECUBA *and* CASSANDRA. HECUBA *is a dignified public figure.*

HECUBA. When I married your father houses had been falling

down in the city for years and no one rebuilt them. There was no money, the mines were empty. I was going to wear something bright, but I thought it ought to be mourning. Lend me your belt. (*She puts on* CASSANDRA's *belt*.) Better . . . I never saw him when he was young. I thought I'd be able to tell what he'd looked like if I saw him asleep. But he looked even older – as if a mask had been pushed through from underneath.

The SON *comes in with the* TROJAN HIGH PRIEST, *the* SECOND TROJAN PRIEST *and the* TROJAN CHAPLAIN.

SON. Say nothing to the Greeks. Just listen.

HECUBA. I shall do anything I can to save the city – not your honour. (*To the* TROJAN PRIESTS.) The plague?

TROJAN HIGH PRIEST. We're praying. It could be over in a month. It's contagious, not infectious. People must sleep and eat and live apart. Mothers can handle children, but children can't play together. Shops are under guard: everyone gets one food ration to prepare on their own.

HECUBA. Are there many dead?

TROJAN HIGH PRIEST. We don't know. It hasn't spread from the poor quarter. We must take strength from our afflictions.

SON. Amen!

HECUBA (*turning away from the* SON). I've begun to hate you young-old people. I'm tired of listening to you argue with your undertakers about the future. Even victory would now cost us more than defeat at the beginning – and what hope is there of victory?

AIDE *comes in.*

AIDE. The Greeks.

THERSITES *and* ISMENE *come in.*

HECUBA (*formally*). I speak for the Trojans.

THERSITES (*formally*). We speak for the Greeks. During the five years the Athenians have been at Troy children have grown to be intelligent youths, gardens have matured, old people have died and their graves been lost in weeds. Return our goddess and we will go without looting, burning or forced labour.

HECUBA. Whoever trusted the Greeks?

THERSITES. The gods have punished you with the plague – but it could spread to us. We want to go.

HECUBA. We have the statue. You say what luck has it brought us? If we give it up what luck could we hope for? That would be your best reason to break your word and destroy us. Perhaps I shall just destroy the statue. God knows, it's not given us much luck –

SON. We'll send our decision when we've –

HECUBA. But you still might not go. I've had five years to study the Greeks. Only a fool would stay for a statue that didn't exist, but only a fool would have sat out there for five years. Who can trust the Greeks?

THERSITES. We swear on the statue.

HECUBA. I feel as if I was talking to visitors from the past: perhaps all this was decided by Priam long ago.

THERSITES. The plague is in the present.

HECUBA. We have a chance against the plague. What chance would we have against the Greeks if we gave you the statue? Our people's will to resist would go. If you had it, would there be any limit to your ferocity? Why should I trust the Greeks? Let me speak to Ismene alone.

THERSITES. That's impossible.

HECUBA. Perhaps two women could find some way of solving this.

THERSITES. It's not possible.

HECUBA. I see! The Greeks don't trust one another but expect the Trojans to trust them.

THERSITES. Wars aren't decided by women talking!

HECUBA. We're talking of peace! Now I insist!

THERSITES. I refuse!

HECUBA. Then I ask . . . for a small thing when you ask me to risk so much

ISMENE. I can only say what he can.

HECUBA. My dear, I don't even know what I wanted to talk to you about. I thought I'd try – in every way I can – to find a solution. That's the duty of all of us here.

THERSITES (*looks at the* SON, *then back to* HECUBA). Well – (*Turns to* ISMENE.) – speak to her.

HECUBA. How sensible even the Greeks can be when they want something. (*Nods to the others.*) Go.

HECUBA *and* ISMENE *are left alone.*

HECUBA. Sit down, my child. (*They both sit.*) Will you take tea?

ISMENE. No thank you.

HECUBA. How long have you been married?

ISMENE. I don't think I quite –

HECUBA. How serious you young people are! Are you always serious?

ISMENE. Seven years. I've laughed in that time.

HECUBA. And no children. Perhaps the goddess of luck would give you children. They say your husband's the most handsome man in the world.

ISMENE. He's often called that.

HECUBA. How nice. Mine was old when I married him. Very old when he died. But we had sons and daughters. I can't imagine what it's like, married to a young man. I'd like to see yours.

ISMENE. I hope you will.

HECUBA. And you miss your mother?

ISMENE. Of course.

HECUBA. There's a good girl! And a lucky one – married to the most handsome man in all the – (*Stops.*) O, I didn't mean – (*She stops again.*) And one day you'll be queen.

ISMENE. Athens is a republic.

HECUBA. Yes, they call you something else. My husband doted on our children. When they went fishing they had to make their rods and lines. And hooks.

ISMENE. How sad that their lives have been wasted.

HECUBA. Tragic. Is that why you asked to come here?

ISMENE. I didn't say I'd asked.

HECUBA. O, your Greek men have sat on my doorstep for five years without having one bright idea. It must have been you.

ISMENE. My husband says Priam stole the statue because you seduced him.

HECUBA. That's not very nice of him.

ISMENE. It wouldn't have been your fault. Leaders should take their own decisions.

HECUBA. O, Priam was a born leader. Cautious – or bold. A good husband. A wise king. But useless. When the old play games they mistake that for youth – it's only senility. Troy is senile. Priam took me to bed . . . to make the city young again. It didn't work. So he stole the statue. That worked for a time. Look how we've resisted you! What other city could have done that? But nothing's changed. Labour for a stillborn child. There . . . I shouldn't have seen you: you've made me tell the truth.

ISMENE. You've been misjudged. But what can I do? Return the statue – then we can leave you in peace.

HECUBA. One good reason?

ISMENE. The plague! Set us free – all of us – and I'll kiss your hand when we go!

HECUBA. Why should I trust your husband?

ISMENE. The Greeks. Athens is a republic.

HECUBA. Your husband.

ISMENE. He's not only handsome – *he's* a born leader. He makes good decisions.

HECUBA. He married you. Though I ask myself why. You're not the most beautiful woman in the world.

ISMENE. No. Now let's talk about what we –

HECUBA. Perhaps you're the wisest? Or the best?

ISMENE. No.

HECUBA. What a pity. At your age I was sensational. A great beauty! I wish you'd seen me. They called me the Venus of Asia. Of course you know that. I can still see it in the glass.

ISMENE. Yes.

HECUBA. As to Athens a republic. Well, your husband's family is the richest in Athens and money buys power. Shall we tell the truth? This is one of those times when a pinch of truth will bring out the full flavour of our lies.

ISMENE. This is too serious to play with words –

HECUBA. Let me show you something. (*She rings a bell.*) If I gave you the statue your husband would still destroy us.

ISMENE. He gives his word.

HECUBA. Yes – and you carry it.

AIDE *comes in.*

HECUBA. Before the war they answered the moment I touched the bell. The Queen of Athens wishes to see my grandson.

AIDE *goes out.*

Your husband will burn Troy to the ground.

ISMENE. Not if you give him the statue!

HECUBA. To the ground!

ISMENE. None of this has ever made sense!

HECUBA. Sense! What has this to do with sense? If men were sensible they wouldn't have to go to war! Is it sensible for the handsomest man in the world to marry the ugliest woman? (ISMENE *stands.*) It's certain that when he married a liar like you there'd be only one result: he'd make you the ugliest woman in the world!

The doors open. CASSANDRA *comes in, leading* ASTYANAX *by the hand.*

CASSANDRA. My son's come to say a nice how-d'you-do to the lady.

ISMENE. Excuse me, I must –

HECUBA. Please don't make a scene in front of the child. One shouldn't frighten children.

CASSANDRA. Go on.

ASTAYANAX. Who is she?

HECUBA. The wife of the Greek leader.

ASTYANAX. Grandma that's naughty.

HECUBA. How my dear?

ASTYANAX. It's bad to play when you're mourning. My tutor told me.

HECUBA. Play my darling?

ASTYANAX. You said she was a Greek. The Greeks are ugly. With long tails and hair between their toes. Ugh! And their breath smells and their eyes are all gummy and when they have a cut black oozes out. My tutor's seen it.

CASSANDRA. Darling, don't talk so much.

ASTYANAX. Perhaps Greek ladies are different from Greek men, mother. But it can't be nice for the Greek ladies. (*To* ISMENE.) Does your husband have hair between his toes? Ugh!

CASSANDRA. Her husband is very handsome.

HECUBA. Kiss me. (ASTYANAX *kisses her.*) Go back to your lessons.

ASTYANAX. Yes, grandma. (*To* ISMENE.) I can make houses out of paper. Goodbye. You're a sad lady.

CASSANDRA. Hush!

ASTYANAX. Are you sad because you'll lose the war? When you're in prison I'll come and show you how to make houses out of paper. Can I grandma?

CASSANDRA. I promised your tutor five minutes.

CASSANDRA *takes* ASTYANAX *out.*

HECUBA. There are thousands of children like my grandson in Troy. Old people like me. Girls like my daughter. In war death's always painful and slow. You wait for it all the time. I give you the statue – my people despair, they already have the plague, and your husband waits at our gates till we give in. Then he enters and butchers!

ISMENE. I give my word!

HECUBA. You know it yet you come here like a pious nun and beg me to set you free – all of us free! Your word? You call me a seducer? You're a whore murdering children to satisfy her clients!

ISMENE. We'll take the statue and go!

HECUBA. Liar!

ISMENE. We will!

HECUBA. Liar! Tell me – under the same roof as that child – your husband will go!

ISMENE. It's easy for you now your husband's dead. Mine's alive. You tell me to make his decisions – but I have no power.

HECUBA. No, I ask you to tell the truth. You could have stayed at home – if someone else's country can be your home – and worried about your dress or the evening meal. I can't make you answer my questions, but I can make you listen to them. If you ignore them you corrupt yourself. We both know the truth: your husband would take the statue and still burn and kill and loot . . . I can't shout any more. My son spends more and more time with the priests. When leaders do that it means you're lost. Shall I give you the statue – so at least some of you go and we can hope to hold out a little longer? Or face the worst now? No, you can take it from our dead hands.

ISMENE. So much trouble will come from this.

HECUBA. I can't see one ray of hope.

ISMENE. I won't go back. Let me stay in Troy.

HECUBA. I haven't asked for that. How will that help us?

ISMENE. I can't go back now we've spoken. Send for Thersites.

HECUBA. I'm sorry – you'll be trapped too.

ISMENE. You must say I'm a hostage. Nothing will be gained if I stay out of shame. Say you'll let me go when they go.

HECUBA. What's the use? They'd come back.

ISMENE. I can't alter everything, but I can do this. Fetch Thersites now – so I can't change my mind. (*She rings.*)

HECUBA. What will your husband do?

ISMENE. I shall see.

AIDE *comes in.*

HECUBA (*nods*). I'm ready.

AIDE *goes out.*

Protest in front of Thersites.

THERSITES, *the* SON, PRIESTS *and* SOLDIERS *come back.*

THERSITES. What have the ladies decided?

HECUBA. I'll give you the statue –

THERSITES. Good!

HECUBA. But there's still one problem: who can trust a Greek? I shall keep Ismene here till you're back in Athens. If you don't go, the priests will cut her throat on the goddess's pedestal – which will be vacant after twenty-five years.

The SON *applauds.*

THERSITES. This is against the laws of war!

ISMENE. It's against all civilized laws.

HECUBA. The goddess sent me these instructions in an oracle. I'm sure your leader will respect that.

THERSITES. I won't leave without Ismene.

HECUBA. You're welcome to our hospitality. I'll send my decision back by runner.

THERSITES. At what stage would you give us the statue?

HECUBA. When you're on your ships.

THERSITES. And Ismene?

HECUBA. I'll keep her till you're back in Athens – or drowned on the way.

THERSITES. Let me speak to Ismene alone.

HECUBA. Certainly.

Everyone except ISMENE *and* THERSITES *leaves.*

THERSITES. Ismene, your husband's position will be very difficult.

ISMENE. So is mine Thersites.

THERSITES. Of course. I meant – Ajax will put pressure – country before self. It's an impossible situation for your husband!

ISMENE. Why? What does the country want? The statue. Now they can have it.

THERSITES. Yes, yes. In politics you always ask for more. If we agree to this, what will they want next? Fools! – why did we let you come? I'll go now and the sooner something can be done. Goodbye.

ISMENE. Goodbye.

> THERSITES *goes. A* SOLDIER *comes on and takes* ISMENE *away.*

FIVE

Greek camp – Headquarters.
NESTOR *and* HEROS.

NESTOR. It could still work out for the best: we could get Ismene and the statue.

HEROS. After they've fortified their coast. With a fortified coast they'd be impregnable. And she could still keep Ismene! What sort of welcome would I get in Athens? Come home with a stone and no wife?

NESTOR. The goddess is certainly testing us.

HEROS. Troy, statue, my wife – in her hands! Now she'd like to make her revenge complete. Get rid of us and throw my wife's body after us in the sea! We're at her mercy! Why why why did I let her go? That woman is a – a –! Athens and Troy can never be at peace! Troy must be destroyed. Stone by stone. If we stay but refuse to talk – would they kill her?

NESTOR. I've seen things done in this war I wouldn't think possible. They're so commonplace we don't notice any more.

HEROS. I can't believe they'd kill her. If they did, I'd kill myself. The moment we had the statue.

NESTOR. Athens will need you even more then. I'd offer my own life.

HEROS. There are seven wonders of the world. What I'll do to Troy will be the first of the seven crimes. Call the council, Nestor.

SIX

Troy – the palace.
HECUBA, ISMENE, *the* SON, THERSITES, PRIESTS *and* SOLDIERS.

THERSITES. You stole the statue of our goddess. Now you've stolen our commander's wife! We stay here till we get both back. All Troy is shamed by this!

HECUBA. My dear child, I'm sorry the Greeks value you less than I do! (*To* THERSITES.) Well at least we have one thing your commander wants: the statue.

SON. Cut off her hair and send it back with this man! Why is she pampered? Let her starve! This woman is a killer of our children! Sparing her even so long shows more humanity than the Greeks will ever have! Yes, go back and tell them the Trojans disagree on some things but agree on this: to use this woman in any way that helps to destroy you! They think they're at war? Tell them the war starts now!

ISMENE. The Trojans are great cooks Thersites. When I'm home in Athens I'll have a Trojan cook in the kitchen. To our taste the food's exotic – but there are many things we can learn. Eat with us before you go. How well everything's worked out! The Trojans will give the Greeks what they want: the statue.

And the Greeks will do what the Trojans want: go. And when they do, I'll follow. Why should the Trojans keep me? The Greeks would come back!

THERSITES. The council will do what's best, Ismene.

ISMENE. O, I'm not putting myself before the best interests of Greece. For once reason –

SON. Heros sent his wife here to get peace at home!

ISMENE. For once reason is on both sides. We shouldn't call this statue the goddess of Good Fortune, but the goddess of good sense.

TROJAN HIGH PRIEST. Sacrilege! I object!

SON. It's said we've offended the goddess and the only way to please her is to kill this woman!

TROJAN HIGH PRIEST. On the goddess's feast day, which falls next Wednesday.

SECOND TROJAN PRIEST. The closeness of that day to the day when the woman fell into our hands is providential.

THERSITES. If that's how you decide strategy I see why you'll lose.

ISMENE. O please don't say –

THERSITES (*admonishing*). Ismene my dear –

ISMENE. I must speak! We're at war so neither side can trust the other. Why shouldn't we give the Trojans a token of our good faith? If it helps, *I* will! I won't go back to my husband till the Greeks go back to Greece. I don't say this lightly. War breeds fanaticism faster than plague. But I trust Hecuba to protect me.

THERSITES. What if she died of the plague? Who'd protect you then, you silly reckless woman. I demand to speak to Ismene alone!

ISMENE. No! We ask to be trusted – we must do nothing in secret!

THERSITES. I'm to go back and tell our council that!

ISMENE. Why not? The Trojans aren't going to send me back just because the council told you to come here and call them naughty! I'll be kept anyway! I'm helping the council by making their choice easier: they can now get all they say they want by being honest! And besides, the Trojan women have a right to ask me for this!

THERSITES. Ismene!

ISMENE. Yes, a right! The Trojan women *expect* you to break your word –

THERSITES. What!

ISMENE. Of course you won't! – but they see you as monsters who've murdered their husbands and fathers! My husband's love for me – the Greeks' love for me – they fight you with *that* because they love their own families! That's almost a good war!

HECUBA. Now try our specialities before you go. I'm sure you're bored with army food.

They all go except the SON *and the* PRIESTS.

TROJAN HIGH PRIEST. Unwise to say so much, sir.

SON. I must speak the truth!

TROJAN HIGH PRIEST. Tchah! Truth's too precious to waste in an argument. The goddess hides the truth. It has to be divined. I've hung a pigeon in a cage high over the city where it sees everything. Tomorrow we'll cut it open and see what it's recorded.

SON. Well what?

The TROJAN CHAPLAIN *is sent out.*

TROJAN HIGH PRIEST. As my life is so close to the goddess I do sometimes hear her whisper. But I must open the pigeon to be sure.

SON. But what?

TROJAN HIGH PRIEST. Doubtless the goddess will say one woman running the country is enough – and she is the woman. She'll pronounce on your mother's – if I may say so – obvious senility, and power will pass to you.

SON. I shall keep the goddess – and her priests. If the Greeks left, who'd come next? Barbarians, savages. My mother doesn't understand this! She thinks she can seduce Mars! With the goddess we can resist all our enemies! I have faith to inspire the people.

TROJAN HIGH PRIEST. When they see the Greek woman humbled their faith will already be strengthened.

They go.

SEVEN

Troy – a prison.

ISMENE *alone. Her hair is shorn, she is pale and in rags.* HECUBA *comes in.*

HECUBA. I watched our behaviour get worse as this war went on. We'll end as barbarians. D'you get enough food?

ISMENE. Yes.

HECUBA. The priests say my mind's gone. They blame it on the burden of office: they mean I've learned from experience. My son's taken over, we'll keep the statue, and Troy will be destroyed. (*Sits.*) I'm in prison too. I eat, sleep and dress as I like, and that's all.

ISMENE. I knew when I came here my husband had lied, but I pretended I didn't. Now he'll build his great new city – but if I lived in it I'd have to pretend all the time. I can't pretend now: that's why I'm in prison. In prison you're free to tell the truth.

HECUBA. My husband blossomed when he was old. He'd stand in the sun for hours like a youth. A wonderful old man's passion. He was like a frail raft on a great river, it gathers all the force from the water and travels so fast. Won't you go back to your husband at all?

ISMENE. You carry a child inside you but you don't choose when it's born. It may come early – or be dead. It lay under your heart as if that were a gravestone. I've been sitting and thinking. I shall speak to the Greeks myself, and tell them to go.

HECUBA. How they've shorn your hair! . . . It won't do any good. I pleaded with my people, and they locked me up.

ISMENE. I shall try.

EIGHT

Greek camp – Headquarters.

HEROS, NESTOR, THERSITES *and* AJAX *sit on stools in council.*

HEROS. The council has the right to decide war matters, but let me decide this.

AJAX. It *is* a war matter.

HEROS. I decide not to give way. The moment we left our lines the Trojans would take the statue up to the mountains. We must stay put now more than ever.

THERSITES. Say we can't decide. Play for time while the plague spreads.

HEROS. No, don't give them one ray of hope. I move next business. Of course my wife's conduct must be kept from the troops.

The others nod. AJAX *goes out and a moment later returns with the* TROJAN HIGH PRIEST *and* SECOND TROJAN PRIEST.

TROJAN HIGH PRIEST. Sir, it's now clear beyond a peradventure that rather than let the goddess pass into your hands Priam's son will destroy her. His impiety horrifies us! Of course the goddess would reincarnate herself –

AJAX. If he destroys her he'll destroy her guardians. Let's hope she reincarnates them!

TROJAN HIGH PRIEST (*to* HEROS). Sir, we're not servants of Troy – or Athens. We serve religion. Let us ask, to whom does the goddess belong? To the Victor! – him she will have blessed with fortune! So, to whoever owns Troy!

HEROS. But how to get Troy!

TROJAN HIGH PRIEST. Priam's son rules Troy while it stands. You can only own its ruins. But when Troy falls – at the moment power slips from his hands – he will destroy the goddess in his sacrilegious fury!

HEROS. Anticipate it and bring her here.

TROJAN HIGH PRIEST. Our duty is worship.

AJAX. Last time you promised to –

TROJAN HIGH PRIEST. No. We said a decision would be made. The goddess decides.

SECOND TROJAN PRIEST. Though that is loosely put. She decides nothing.

TROJAN HIGH PRIEST. True. Admirable man! It was decided long ago.

SECOND TROJAN PRIEST. The goddess merely *sees*.

AJAX. What does she see?

TROJAN HIGH PRIEST. She hasn't said.

HEROS. Goddam!

TROJAN HIGH PRIEST. You haven't put yourself in the place where her light can fall on you. Just as the humblest suppliant wanting to know when to open his shop or sow his corn, must make the right offering – so must the great of this world.

HEROS. What offering?

TROJAN HIGH PRIEST. We slaughtered many pigeons to be sure. The answer is always clear: the ruins of Troy.

HEROS (*sighs, then bursts out angrily*). Troy Troy Troy Troy! I wish I'd never heard the name! Why has my wife refused to come back?

TROJAN HIGH PRIEST. An impious woman, sir – with respect.

THERSITES. Who forced her?

TROJAN HIGH PRIEST. No one.

NESTOR. I don't believe it!

SECOND TROJAN PRIEST. Even peacocks' entrails couldn't explain her.

HEROS. It was Hecuba!

> *The* SECOND TROJAN PRIEST *tugs the* TROJAN HIGH PRIEST*'s sleeve.*

TROJAN HIGH PRIEST. We must go while it's dark.

> *The* TROJAN HIGH PRIEST *and the* SECOND TROJAN PRIEST *go out.*

HEROS. When the dust of Troy finally goes up they'll have a moment of power. The statue is in their hands.

NESTOR. My boy, if what those priests say about your wife is true, she's put you in a terrible position. The ancient punishment for treason in time of war is fixed: common women burned and ladies immured. Your wife is in danger of being walled up alive in the ruins of Troy.

Commotion outside.

HEROS. What now?

AIDE *comes in.*

AIDE. Sir –

The GREEK HIGH PRIEST, SECOND GREEK PRIEST *and* GREEK CHAPLAIN *force their way in past him.*

GREEK HIGH PRIEST. Sir, there was no doubt! Trojan priests seen entering and leaving this council. We must ask for an –

HEROS. We're trying to get them to smuggle the statue out.

GREEK HIGH PRIEST. Sir, when the goddess is ours you'll let Trojan priests attend her? Look at the state of Troy! That shows what use they are!

SECOND GREEK PRIEST. Amen!

GREEK HIGH PRIEST. The goddess speaks Greek – in the spiritual sense.

GREEK CHAPLAIN (*low*). The goddess speaks Greek in the spiritual sense.

GREEK HIGH PRIEST. The Greek eternity speaking to the Greek temporality.

GREEK CHAPLAIN (*low*). The Greek eternity speaking to the Greek temporality.

GREEK HIGH PRIEST. Bless you, brother! (*To* HEROS.) The Greek Hierarchy alone –

GREEK CHAPLAIN (*low*). The Greek Hierarchy alone –

GREEK HIGH PRIEST. Yes, yes – thank you, brother! –

GREEK CHAPLAIN. Yes, yes – thank you, brother! –

HEROS. I've no intention of allowing Trojan priests to serve in Athens. They've protected the Trojan theft up to the last. I imagine the Athenian parliament will vote to stone them to death outside the city walls.

GREEK HIGH PRIEST. Ah! But the Trojan priests don't know this.

GREEK CHAPLAIN. – know this.

HEROS. They have a good idea. That's why the negotiations take so long.

GREEK HIGH PRIEST. O Athens will be blessed with this captain at the helm! Brothers let us sweep the temple and give thanks!

SECOND GREEK PRIEST. Amen!

GREEK CHAPLAIN. – give thanks!

GREEK HIGH PRIEST. We tell our soldiers how wisely they're led.

GREEK CHAPLAIN. – they're led.

They all go.

NINE

Battleground in front of the Trojan wall.
ISMENE *comes on, escorted by Trojan soldiers.*

ISMENE. Greek soldiers! Go home! Is there any loot worth the risk of your life? Women? There are women in Greece! The goddess? If the Trojans listened to me they'd throw it out to you over their wall. That's how they'd punish you most! What luck could it give you? You'll go home when you've got it? You can go home now! You're wasting your life making your tombstone! (*She starts to move on.*) No one answers: there *is* no answer.

NESTOR *comes on with an* AIDE *and the* CAPTAIN.

NESTOR. Ismene your husband's at home with the doors and windows bolted. He can't face his shame. He knows you're forced but he commands you to stop whatever the cost. Obey him!

ISMENE. Nestor, you're old enough to set these young men an example. If you don't go soon you'll never see Greece.

NESTOR. I'm not a traitor!

ISMENE. Soldiers I've heard Nestor in council. They say, find out what Nestor thinks and then do the opposite.

NESTOR. Ismene, you're insulting! (*He turns and shouts back to the Greek lines.*) She's off her head!

ISMENE. Soldiers, I speak to you, not your leaders. They have everything at stake here. If they lose Athens will throw them out.

NESTOR. Soldiers, she says these things – these ravings! – to *prove* she's being forced. We understand the code, Ismene! Go on! Very good dear!

ISMENE. Who needs to be led to food? Or warmth? Or shelter? You only need leaders to lead you astray! The good shepherd leads his sheep to the butcher!

NESTOR. Soldiers, I forbid you to listen!

ISMENE. Go home! Then you've won the war!

NESTOR. She's mad! (*To* AIDE *and* CAPTAIN.) Clap! Make a noise! Noise! Noise!

> NESTOR, AIDE *and* CAPTAIN *stamp, clap and beat their weapons.* ISMENE *shouts over them.*

More!

NESTOR, AIDE and CAPTAIN. Hooooo! Hooooo! Hooooo!

ISMENE. What happens when you get to Athens? The shepherd will still fleece his sheep! They're in your hands now. You have weapons. In Athens they'll take your weapons away! (*She moves on.*) Soldiers you'll never get the statue! The Trojans will break it to pieces!

NESTOR (*to* AIDE *and* CAPTAIN). Shut up, shut that row up! (*They are quiet. He shouts to* ISMENE.) We can *prove* that's a lie! Even the Trojans wouldn't destroy that holy statue: their land would be cursed and laid waste!

ISMENE. It's already laid waste!

NESTOR. Noise!

> NESTOR *gestures to the* AIDE *and* CAPTAIN. *All three go off making a noise.* ISMENE *walks on round the walls.*

Priam's city has nothing to give you but a grave and rubble to fill it! Soldiers, nothing but a grave and rubble to fill it! A grave and rubble! Soldiers a grave and rubble!

> ISMENE *and her escort go out.*

TEN

Troy – the palace.
PRIESTS *and* HECUBA.

TROJAN HIGH PRIEST. Ma'am we've been to the Greek leaders.
HECUBA. I wondered when you would.
TROJAN HIGH PRIEST. Hear us, ma'am. At last the viscera are clear. The goddess's time for passing to the Greeks has come. People with plague are wandering about in delirium. The soldiers refuse to cut any more down. The poor are rioting. We can't maintain order in the city or defeat our enemies outside.
HECUBA. You gave my son power.
TROJAN HIGH PRIEST. Cut him down like a dog!
SECOND TROJAN PRIEST. The goddess decrees it!
TROJAN HIGH PRIEST. Sacrilege takes strange forms in the young. Your son wants us to be defeated! – to have the pleasure of attacking the goddess with an axe!
HECUBA. If I take power I shall give the statue to the Greeks. And they may still destroy us.
TROJAN HIGH PRIEST. Not the college of priests. Heros is unsure. He'll protect us – not out of reverence but superstition. We'll make you high priestess.

> *The* SON *enters with* SOLDIERS.

SON. My mother with the traitors.

TROJAN HIGH PRIEST. Sir! We came to beg her to join our prayers for victory!

SON. I've had visitors: the Greek priests.

TROJAN HIGH PRIEST. Sir, the goddess has spoken against you! Submit!

SECOND TROJAN PRIEST. Return the statue –

TROJAN CHAPLAIN. Demand mercy –

SON. Would the Greeks listen? They speak only one language: sword sword sword!

HECUBA. What else can we do?

SON. We can fight and die or surrender and die. All the arguing and scheming was for one thing: how each of us saved his neck. But it's always been clear we won or died together. No exceptions were ever possible. And now I think because we didn't stand close, our chances aren't worth *that*! So let us see. Take those priests out in the street. Now! See what *their* entrails say in the gutter. I am the priest now! I'll come and interpret their offal!

TROJAN PRIESTS. Please! Please! We spoke to the Greeks on the goddess's command! She sent us! To persuade them!

SON. The street!

TROJAN PRIESTS. The negotiations are almost finished! Let us complete it!

SOLDIERS *take the* TROJAN PRIESTS *out.*

SON. I'm honester than you, mother. You want to take a chance with the Greeks: but you know it doesn't exist. I won't even bother to take it. I'm not your enemy, mother. I'll fight for you and the city. That stone – is only a stone. A goddess wouldn't let those sewer rats pester her! Not if she had the insight of an idiot! I'm so tired today. I prayed and worked for this time – when I threw Troy against Greece. Now it's come when I'm weak. The weight of this war, the plague and the city, crushed me. My life is like a stone I could spit out of my mouth.

HECUBA. I saw this war corrupt almost everyone it touched. It's taken you to the limit of corruption.

HECUBA *starts to go.*

SON. No doubt. I'm off to the temple to weep and wail and inspire the people. I shall be the man who stands on the street corner of history with a rope round his neck and beckons the spectators to come and be hanged.

ELEVEN

Battle ground in front of the Trojan walls.
ISMENE *wanders on with her Trojan escort. She is tired and dirty. From the Greek lines an uproar of rattled spears, shields and tins and rhythmically shouted orders and clapping.*

ISMENE. Soldiers, nothing but a grave and rubble to fill it! Peace! Peace! Peace!
GREEK SOLDIERS (*off*). Traitoress! Traitoress! Traitoress!
ISMENE. You'll be thrown into a grave on top of women and children you killed. Rubble from the ruins you make will be thrown on top of you! Soldiers peace! Peace! Peace!

ISMENE *wanders off with her escort. The uproar dies.*

TWELVE

Troy – temple precinct
A few respectable BYSTANDERS, *sniffing nosegays and stuffed oranges against the plague. The* SON *with a phalanx of* SOLDIERS. *He prepares to enter the temple.*

SOLDIERS. Goddess of Fortune
     Sharpen the sword
     Weight the axe
     Guide the spear
     Deep in the joint
     Of the neck armour

BYSTANDERS (*sniffing nosegays and oranges*). Praise the goddess. May the goddess be praised. Let the goddess bless the people.

SON. Goddess of Fortune
     You took away your blessing
     When false priests served you
     We purify your temple with our tears

BYSTANDERS (*sniffing nosegays and oranges*). Down with the Greeks. Death to Athens. Death to their leaders. The destruction of Athens.

SON (*holding up a blood-stained sword*).
     Goddess of Fortune
     Who punished the false priests with plague
     Accept their blood on this sword
     And give us victory!

BYSTANDERS (*sniffing nosegays and oranges*). Cleanse the water. Heal the sick. Feed the poor. Protect the law. Open the markets.

The SON *begins to mount the steps to the temple. A crowd comes on: the poor, starved, wounded, sick, lame, crazed. Some have early symptoms of plague. They are all filthy and in rags.*

CROWD. Food! Water! Heal us! We're starving! Alms! Bread! My wife's dead! My son! Plague! Money! Help us!

The SON *and the* BYSTANDERS *are forced to back up the temple steps.*

SON (*on the top of the steps*). Trojans! Goddess! Friends!
CROWD. Death!

SON *is stabbed from behind. He falls down the steps. The crowd rush into the temple. The* SOLDIERS *and* BYSTANDERS *creep towards the dead* SON.

FIRST BYSTANDER (*peering and sniffing a nosegay*). Us next.
FIRST SOLDIER. Time to run.
SECOND SOLDIER. The only chance.
SECOND and THIRD BYSTANDERS (*to* SOLDIERS). No. No. Help us.
FOURTH BYSTANDER. What good could we do if we stayed?

The SOLDIERS *and* BYSTANDERS *hurry off. The crowd pours out of the temple. They carry the statue of the goddess high over their heads. A plain, grey, schematized female shape, of worn but not smooth stone, about three-quarters life-size, exaggerated in length not thickness.*

CROWD. Out! Out! Out! Throw her out! Chuck her out! Get rid of her! Out Out! Out! Bitch! Bitch! Bitch! No more bitch! Out!

The BEGGARS *spin, stamp, shout, chant, laugh, cry – but above all dance and sing. A* BEGGAR *collapses. Some clutch themselves and each other in pain and excitement. Some wave rags like flags and handkerchiefs. The figure is jostled along high over their heads.*

Wait! Wait! Listen! (*Noise subsides for a moment.*) Let the Greeks have her! They deserve her! To the Greeks! Throw her out! We're throwing the goddess out! No more Bitch! Bitch out! Plague out! War out! Famine out! Out! Out! Out! To the Greeks!

The crowd jostle out with the statue. Sick BEGGARS *limp off after them. They stumble and fall as they try to catch up. Others run into the temple. Others carry the* SON *out, pulling at his clothes and giggling. The stage is empty.*

THIRTEEN

Greek camp – Headquarters.
NESTOR, THERSITES, HEROS *and other* OFFICERS *assembling as a court.*

NESTOR. You're tired.
HEROS. I've walked through Troy.
NESTOR. Shall I postpone the hearing?
HEROS. Get it over.
NESTOR. What procedure? The oldest member usually presides.
HEROS. Just as normal.
NESTOR. There's no need for you to take part.
HEROS. I said as normal! (*Calmer.*) I can't break the law and then build a new city of justice!

> AJAX *comes in and reports to* HEROS.

AJAX. The city's ready for tomorrow. There'll be no fighting amongst ourselves – each regiment's got its own area. The palace loot is being shipped out now.
NESTOR. I'd rather have gone away empty-handed than face this.

> NESTOR *and the others sit on their stools.* ISMENE *is brought in by a* GUARD. *She wears dress clothes and jewels.*

NESTOR. Sit down. (*She sits.*) In one way the case against you's clear. The whole Greek army heard you commit treason day after day. What isn't clear, to some, is why. Yet I suppose that's also clear. You were a hostage trying to save her life – right and proper in a woman. The fault lies with some of our council for sending you.
FIRST OFFICER. Do we lead our men to the butchers?
NESTOR (*interrupting*). One moment.
SECOND OFFICER. Favouritism!
FIRST OFFICER. This woman belongs to the highest rank in our society!

SECOND OFFICER. She attacked us in front of our men!

THIRD OFFICER. Ask her what she thinks now!

NESTOR. I run this court and ask the questions! (*To* ISMENE.) Now, isn't what I've said true?

ISMENE. I don't wish to quarrel with my city. But I have only one life – and so there's only one way I can live it. That's why I'm afraid.

AJAX. Answer the question. Do we mislead our men?

ISMENE. I am a Greek –

OFFICERS *applaud ironically*.

ISMENE. – and speak the truth as far as I can –

OFFICERS. Answer! Answer! Answer!

NESTOR. Order!

AJAX. The things you said – were they true?

OFFICERS. Answer!

ISMENE. Soldiers have died who would be living now if –

OFFICERS. Sentence!

NESTOR. I see! You're ashamed you were weak in Troy, so you're brave here. That's easier – you know we're more merciful than those fanatics. Ismene, this is weakness too – you make yourself a traitor twice over. This show of strength comes too late. We'd forget your insults to Greek men. But now you're insulting Greek women! You show the world one of them defying her husband in open court.

ISMENE. Nestor, the world's changed since you learned to talk like that. Your subtlety sounds silly.

OFFICERS. Shame! Sentence!

THERSITES. You say these things because you're safe. The punishment for treason – no one would ask for that barbarous sentence –

ISMENE. No one ask? The Greeks not barbarous? I shall speak the truth!

THERSITES. What truth?

ISMENE. In Troy I saw the people suffer. Young men crippled or

killed, their parents in despair and dying of disease. I told them
as they were dying – they couldn't hear but I told them because
I'm Greek! – I shall do all I can to stop this. No more suffering
caused by men! I said that – if the sight of them hadn't made
my mouth dry I would have sung it! Yes! And now tomorrow:
tomorrow you'll go into the city – the frightened people are
spending their last night in their homes – and you schoolboys
will prowl through the streets looking for something left to steal
or kill. Is that Greek?

NESTOR. They'd do the same to us.

AJAX. Our men are entitled to their day!

OFFICERS. Hear hear!

ISMENE. Entitled?

AJAX. I demand the full sentence on this woman!

OFFICERS. Sentence! Sentence!

ISMENE. Ajax the boy demands! My turn! All of you: me next!

NESTOR. Be quiet! I will not tolerate this!

OFFICERS. Sentence!

> HEROS *stands. The shouting dies down.*

HEROS. You have no doubts?

ISMENE. I have many doubts – I – (*She stops.*) I wanted someone
wiser than me to speak.

> Some OFFICERS *laugh.*

SECOND OFFICER (*to* THIRD OFFICER). Is your wife wise?

THIRD OFFICER. How could I know?

> Some OFFICERS *laugh.*

HEROS. Why did you say you'd have sung those things?

ISMENE. Sung? I don't think I said I'd – (*She stops again.*)
I only know what I saw!

HEROS. If you have doubts, why are you so defiant?

ISMENE. I'm not defiant!

HEROS. You're defiant.

ISMENE. But if I say what I saw –

HEROS. And prouder than any soldier. You were the one Greek in Troy. You'd only seen war from a hill top –

ISMENE. O I've known since I married you –

NESTOR. Don't interrupt!

HEROS. You were under great stress. You suffered like someone under torture.

ISMENE. Not as much.

HEROS. I won't quarrel. But you suffered.

ISMENE. Yes.

NESTOR. In that case the court can see its way to –

ISMENE. But I shall suffer more tomorrow!

THERSITES. Ismene, we're trained – we train ourselves – not to suffer in that way. If we did we couldn't do our work.

ISMENE. Precisely!

NESTOR. She says precisely as if something had been cleared up, and she's only made it more muddled.

ISMENE. Tomorrow – tomorrow leave Troy alone. Troy has –

NESTOR. She's started again. Clearly you're still under stress. I hand you over to your husband's keeping. Under his care you'll recover from your ordeal.

ISMENE. Tomorrow – don't go to Troy. They say war turns women into prophets. I will prophesy. You have your goddess of Good Fortune. Let her do her worst! I passed the statue out on the square when I came here. The soldiers had carried her there with blood on their hands. You could see the shape of their hands where they'd held her. I curse every Greek who goes into Troy! I curse him and his house! Young soldiers were sharpening knives and swords on the square. They were pumping the pedals like laughing schoolboys. The great army sand-stones whirled round and round. They'd started to drink – at least some of them will be too sick to go! They jumped on the pedals in excitement and the stones screamed like children.

During this speech the OFFICERS *have broken up, talked among themselves and played army games. Only* NESTOR, THERSITES *and* HEROS *have remained in their places.*

HEROS (*calmly*). I ask the court to be allowed to speak to my wife alone. I want to persuade her to apologise to the court, or at least be quiet.

NESTOR. Ismene, your husband's a good, wise man. That makes it even more painful.

The court clears. ISMENE *and* HEROS *are left alone.*

HEROS. One starving child and all your love goes. We don't love because things go well, we love because everything's against it. I've seen sights you can't imagine: I won't tell you about them. If I left Troy tomorrow, Troy would attack us – or someone else would attack Troy. When will there be peace? When we honour virtue and are hungry for simplicity. That won't come overnight. But the new Athens will stand for that. It will produce its own quarrels and its critics. But when people suffer they'll remember Athens. It will be the last thing many people will see before they go mad.

ISMENE. Troy's like a wounded animal. It can't run away. Yet you'll bend over and watch it while you mutilate it!

HEROS. We've given Troy every reason to hate us. There must be no more Trojans to carry on this war. Ismene, I've made love to you but you're still a virgin. If the army raped you on the street corners of Troy tomorrow, you'd still be a virgin. You receive nothing – you only give. All women are virgins when they're faced with murder – perhaps that's why soldiers murder them. They'll brick you up with three days' food – to give you time to repent before you meet the judges of the underworld. I'll see it's poisoned. Eat it as soon as you're walled in. When Troy's destroyed you'll be in a world where the gods don't raise their voices. You can look down on us with their dispassion.

ISMENE. Many people die saying what I've said. Who are they? Who killed them? How many more will die – and who'll know?

If I were free tomorrow to curse the Greeks when they went into Troy – then I'd be remembered.

HEROS. You'd be a sideshow. A parody of the real truth.

ISMENE. I'm a virgin? You want to be an innocent murderer! Burn and kill – the victims are dead, the soldiers are too drunk on wine and violence to remember – it will all disappear the next day. No, I shan't kill myself. I'll be alive when you go into Troy. I shall sit in the dark and listen till the last wail. Not to tell tales when I go to heaven, but so that the truth is recorded on earth.

FOURTEEN

The Trojan wall
The wall is ruined – a gap, half-filled with rubble, leads to a road into the city, which is off left. CASSANDRA, ASTYANAX and TROJAN WOMEN sit and lie on the right. Each has a refugee bundle. ISMENE is bricked into the wall on the left. ARTOS, CRIOS and the CAPTAIN guard her.

FIRST WOMAN. It's still afternoon.

SECOND WOMAN. But late.

FIRST WOMAN. The city's quiet. They're killing the old people.

CASSANDRA (*covering ASTYANAX's ears gently*). I must wash your hair.

ARTOS. Tap.

    CRIOS *taps the wall.*

(*To* CRIOS.) Enough jewellery on her to keep me in luxury if I live to be a thousand.

    ASTYANAX *goes to the gap in the wall.*

CASSANDRA. Where are you going?

ASTYANAX. To see the city.

CASSANDRA. Sit down.

ASTYANAX. It'll be gone tomorrow. (*He starts to walk back.*) Will
we go on the ship tonight? How long will it take to burn the
city?

SECOND WOMAN. Keep your child quiet!

THIRD WOMAN. We want to listen!

ASTYANAX (*whisper*). Where's grandma?

CASSANDRA. She'll be here soon.

ASTYANAX. Will we go in a big ship?

SECOND WOMAN. Please keep your child quiet!

CASSANDRA. I'm sorry. (*To* ASTYANAX.) Try to sleep. (*To*
SECOND WOMAN.) The boy's nervous.

ASTYANAX. Don't want to sleep. Have horrid dreams.

CASSANDRA. You must be a good boy tomorrow and help your
mother.

> HEROS *and* THERSITES *come on.*

HEROS. These woman had water?

CAPTAIN. Mid-day, sir. We searched the bundles, sir.

> AJAX, SOLDIERS *and* GREEK PRIESTS *bring the statue through
> the gap in the wall. It's draped and garlanded. The* GREEK
> PRIESTS *swing incense and some of them carry loot.*

GREEK HIGH PRIEST. Bow! Bow! Bow!

SOLDIERS. Goddess! Goddess! Goddess!

GREEK HIGH PRIEST. Trojans bow too!

GREEK CHAPLAIN. Bow too!

> *A* TROJAN WOMAN *spits on the ground in front of her.*

AJAX. Let the snake spit!

HEROS. Greeks – honour our goddess for the Victory!

SOLDIERS. Victory! Victory! Victory to Athens! Athens!
Athens!

ISMENE (*in the wall*). I heard children running to warn their parents: Greeks! Then soldiers running after them. Racing to get the first child. Seeing who threw him highest. (*General confusion.* CAPTAIN *bangs on the wall.*) Then the soldiers kicked in the doors and threw loot down to the priests from the windows.

GREEK PRIESTS (*angrily to the* SOLDIERS). Chant! Chant! Chant!

SOLDIERS. Goddess of Fortune
    Hail!
    Who sharpened the blade
    And guided the axe through the helmet
    Hail!

The PRIESTS *go to one side with the statue.*

HEROS. Delirium!

AJAX. O those cunning Trojans! Every house – money under the floors, up the chimneys, in the yard!

 HECUBA *comes through the gap. She has two* WOMEN ATTEN-DANTS *with her.* SOLDIERS *whistle and jeer.*

CASSANDRA. Mother!

HECUBA. I stayed with our people to the end. (CASSANDRA *and her* TWO ATTENDANTS *try to help her over the rubble. She pushes them back.*) I can walk . . . (*Sees* HEROS.) O Heros, I won't shout and curse. You great wise man, let me kneel at your feet and learn.

HEROS. What!

HECUBA. Teach me. Not how to herd women through the streets and goad them with your swords so you can chase them, or how to jeer when the old run and fall down, or how to mock when you lean over them with your sword, or kill a woman and wipe the knife in her husband's grey beard, or throw a man's blood down on his own doorstep – not all these skills of violence –

HEROS. The Trojans owe all this to you.

HECUBA. – but how to tell between right and wrong. You must be wise, to know that. We had a library in Troy but I never found it – and you've burned the library now. Philosophers hunted for centuries – came to us from the whole world – but they couldn't tell me. Now here is the man who can! No one would license so much murder and not know the answer.

HEROS. Troy would have done the same!

HECUBA. Troy would have been wrong! Is that the lesson? No, teach me more! You great destroyer – now be Troy's bene-factor! Teach us the meaning of justice! I've come from the ruins of my city to ask. If you can't teach me the –

HEROS. Your young men were killed in the war. No problem. Middle-aged – men and women – will be shipped to the mines. Unwanted child-bearing women died in today's action. You and your daughter will go to Greece – with your own women. Your conditions will be tolerable. The child must be killed.

CASSANDRA. No.

HEROS. Now. It's better over. (*Motions to the* SOLDIERS.)

CASSANDRA. No. No. Please.

HECUBA. You won't pollute your swords on a child?

HEROS. Throw him off the wall – (*Indicates off-stage to the* SOLDIERS.) where it's high.

CASSANDRA. No. No.

WOMEN. Please.

HEROS. Quickly.

WOMEN (*crying*). Please. No.

HECUBA. No. No. Don't – I shall be blamed. I provoked you. I was wrong. Don't burden me with this! Forgive me! You see the state I'm in. Look – I say please. You've made me humble now. Take him to Greece. Bring him up an Athenian.

ASTYANAX. Grandma!

HEROS (*gestures to the* SOLDIERS. *To the* WOMEN). Let the child go.

HECUBA. Teach him to hate us. Tell him I stole the statue. Say I ruined Troy. Heros think of the ways you can gratify your hate! Teach him I'm a whore!

HEROS. Women give them that child!

WOMEN. No! He's our only child. Our son. The rest are dead. Leave us this child. We're all his mother. Don't kill our son, you'd kill hundreds of children at one blow. Make a hundred women childless!

HECUBA. If the stones could speak!

HEROS (*to* SOLDIERS). Take it!

    The WOMEN *cry.*

HECUBA. Think of the cruelty you'll have! Watch him thrown from the wall? Phoosh! – a waste! A sack of rubbish thrown through the air! It's gone! Take him to Athens – teach him to imitate Priam to entertain your friends – teach him to hate me – his mother. When you're old and can't even lift your sword to admire it – he'll stand by your bedside and curse Troy – talk filth about us. Even your old age will be gratified. Your last bed will be a place of lust!

ISMENE (*in the wall*). Heros let the child go!

HECUBA. I have appealed to him in the name of God and the devil! What can I do?

AJAX. She's mad.

ISMENE (*in the wall*). Heros, listen!

HECUBA. What! There! Listen – the ground spoke! Yes – speak – speak!

ISMENE (*in the wall*). Take the child! Make him our son!

HECUBA. There – again! It spoke! (*To* HEROS – *laughing.*) Now you will listen!

    The WOMEN *cry.*

THIRD WOMAN. His wife.

HECUBA. What?

SECOND WOMAN. His wife.

THIRD WOMAN. In the wall.

HECUBA. His wife? There? In there! Who is this monster?

HEROS. I will not stop today. In this war there's been death – from every angle! We all saw it! Now you! He'll die and you'll see his body!

HECUBA. Now that is a simple lesson – and I have learned it!

> HECUBA *turns and goes back through the gap with her* TWO ATTENDANTS. *The other* WOMEN *weep.*

AJAX. Stop her!

HEROS. Let her go! Find a beam and hang yourself! Did you leave a beam for her? Be patient? – wait one minute so you have time to think? I waited five years! She had five years to save him – and all the rest, all of you have five years! The lives lost here – I waste them for the sake of one child? That's mercy? Those soldiers buried in the ground – if the ground could speak it would use their voice and say No! I sum up this war today. I won't feel shame for that!

> *During this the* SOLDIERS *have taken* ASTYANAX *out. The* WOMEN *screamed and then cried.*

CASSANDRA. Since his father was killed he's often played at soldiers with his friends. They pretended to die on the wall. (*She starts to go towards the gap.*) Let me go to him. Please. My little boy with the strangers. He's not used to being handled roughly. (*A* SOLDIER *bars her way.*) Let me kiss him once. While he can see me. Not when he's dead. Let me stroke his hair. Please. (*She goes back to the* WOMEN *crying.*) This world is cruel. If the whole sky was a cloth and I wrapped it round my wound the blood would soak through in one moment. I cannot bear this. I don't know how.

> *Off, one scream.*

THERSITES. I'll see.

HEROS. Let her hang. Like a criminal on a gibbet. I won't have her buried.

> *Hecuba's* TWO ATTENDANTS *run on through the gap and sit down with the other* WOMEN.

THE TWO ATTENDANTS. The queen . . . The queen . . .

HECUBA *screams, off.*

WOMAN (*off*). The queen! The queen!

HECUBA comes through the gap. She has blinded herself.

HECUBA. Where? Where? Where? Show him my face. Women point me out. The man who killed my son. Look. Look.

The WOMEN *groan. More* WOMEN *appear in the gap behind* HECUBA *and watch. The* GREEK PRIESTS *rush out with the statue.*

FIRST ATTENDANT. Our mistress has blinded herself.

HECUBA. Who's there?

ISMENE (*in the wall*). Is Troy burning? I don't understand this sound.

HECUBA (*groping*). Show him my face! Let that man see my face! Where? Where? Fetch that man-child to my feet and make him see my face!

HEROS. Bitch!

HECUBA. What? What is –? I see him in my head! (*She rubs her eyes with her hair.*) Him! Still there! Is there no way to put him out of sight? (*She walks towards HEROS, pointing at him.*) He's in my head! There!

HEROS. Bitch!

AJAX. Bitch!

THERSITES. Bitch!

SOLDIERS. Bitch!

The MEN *draw their swords to protect themselves.*

HECUBA (*stops*). It speaks! There! I see! This eye – all of you – (*Pointing.*) There – there! (*Calls to her* ATTENDANTS.) Shallios! Where is my knife! I have one eye! Quickly! My courage will go! I must be blind!

AJAX, THERSITES. Bitch!

HEROS. Take her! Bitch! All of them! The ships! Burn the city! Now! Now! Men to the ships! Burn it!

The SOLDIERS *run the* WOMEN *out – they help some of them with their bundles.* HEROS, AJAX *and* THERSITES *go through the gap towards the city.*

ARTOS (*tense*). Captain?

CAPTAIN (*tense*). You wait till the last ship. Deal with stragglers. Don't worry: there's a nice pile of loot on one side for you lot on duty today.

CRIOS. Good old captain.

The CAPTAIN *goes out through the gap.* NESTOR *comes on through the gap with* TWO SOLDIERS. *All three are drunk, oily, dirty and bloody. They carry bundles of loot.*

NESTOR. Well boys the last city I'll sack! I ran up the streets like a lad, didn't I?

FIRST SOLDIER. You did, sir.

NESTOR. I drank and swore and sang and waved my sword like a lad. I held the girls for the boys. Didn't I?

SECOND SOLDIER. You did old grandad.

NESTOR. And my god if I didn't have loot on my back like a common soldier I'd have had strength for the women too!

FIRST SOLDIER. You would sir!

NESTOR. Ha ha I would!

FIRST SOLDIER. They love a long beard.

NESTOR. I can reek my youth on me now! Snff! I can smell my manhood again. Smell! Smell!

NESTOR *holds out his arm to be smelt.*

FIRST SOLDIER. Like the dustbin of a brothel sir.

NESTOR (*puts on a Trojan helmet and waves his sword*). Rah! Rah! Wasn't I brave lads! I skipped like a goat. Blood on the sword at my age! What? I showed some of my generation to the grave!

SECOND SOLDIER. You're one of us sir.

NESTOR (*looks at the helmet*). Chopped chap's head off – then shook it out the helmet. I've got a thirst on me boys. I could drink the sea and piss out salt!

SECOND SOLDIER (*offers* NESTOR *his wine*). Try some of the best sir! (NESTOR *drinks and dabs his forehead.*) My Gods I've been with the greats today! I'll have stories to tell when I've got a beard grandad.

NESTOR. Yes, my boy, we were all with the greats today. With the heroes whose mirror is the sea, and whose hair is the yellow shore. O lads let us remember the solemnity of the world and the awfulness of war.

FIRST and SECOND SOLDIERS. Yes old father.

NESTOR. And that we're mortal.

SECOND SOLDIER. And drunk.

FIRST SOLDIER. In the morning, it's Greece and home and –

NESTOR. No. I sail tonight. At my age the days count. I shall look back at Troy burning – with this wind there'll be a bonfire! – the sky and the sea red. Then far out – there's a good wind – the fires will die down and the sea turn black. I shall see the stars. In the morning there'll be a smudge of smoke on the horizon. And I'll turn my face to Greece. You smell the olives before you see the land, as if they could root in the water. Now lads, down to the shore – and make our sacrifice.

> *The* TWO SOLDIERS *support* NESTOR *as they go out.* TROY *starts to burn.*

ARTOS. Glad I'm not on board with them tonight.

SECOND SOLDIER. Let me sir. (*Takes* NESTOR's *bundle.*)

NESTOR. Thank you son. My boy.

> NESTOR *and the two* SOLDIERS *go.*

ARTOS. Tap again.

CRIOS (*taps wall. Calls.*) Hey? (*No answer.*)

ARTOS. Go on.

> CRIOS *taps again. No answer.*

Part Two

An island. The shore of sand slopes upstage to the sea. Left, a low wooden hut. On the edge of the sea, right, flat rocks and a path to the beach.

ONE

Spring.
Music, off. A crowd of fishing villagers come on. The women carry a few loaves and the men a platter of fish. They place them on the flat rocks. ISMENE *leads* HECUBA *from the hut.* HECUBA *has an eye-plug bound to her head by a band.* TEMI, *the chief villager, and his wife* PORPOISE, *both middle-aged, supervise the festival.*

PORPOISE. Boys here, girls here. (*To* HECUBA *and* ISMENE.) Further back.
BOYS (*sing*).   Fish from the sea
               White bread from the oven
               The green green mountain
               For the hairy goat

               Goat skin on my shoulder
               Fire laughs on the hearth
               Bread smiles in the oven
               God throws his net
               To fish! Fish! Fish!

The GIRLS *dance. From time to time the* BOYS *shout in unison* 'To fish! Fish! Fish!' *The* OLDER VILLAGERS *watch. All the* VILLAGERS *cheer when the dance ends. They laugh at* TWO OLD WOMEN *imitating the girls' dance.*

PORPOISE. The race is ready!

VILLAGERS. The race! The race!
PORPOISE. Here! Here!

The boys line up. One is ahead of the others.

GEMIL (*a young girl*). Orvo cheats!
PORPOISE. To the back! Right back!

ORVO *goes to the back. The* VILLAGERS *laugh.*

ISMENE. She's sent someone to the back!
PORPOISE. Off!

The BOYS *race off. The* GIRLS *follow. The* OLDER VILLAGERS *gather together.*

OLDER VILLAGERS.   Sun
　　　　　　　　 Bright steersman of water
　　　　　　　　 Watch the race
　　　　　　　　 And the runners' return!

The OLDER VILLAGERS *follow the younger ones out.* HECUBA *and* ISMENE *are alone.* HECUBA *starts to go down to the beach.*

ISMENE (*looking off*). They're running up the hill. In front of the harbour. So steep!
VILLAGERS (*off, in the distance*). Hyspos! Orvo! Alios! Faster! Not so fast! He'll run out of breath! (*Laughter and the shouting of names fades.*)
ISMENE. How did I lose my mind?
HECUBA. I've told you so many times. You can't remember.
ISMENE. Tell me!
HECUBA. You child. The islanders let us live here and give us food. You're my eyes – and I make you eat, and wash, and rock you to sleep when you're afraid.
ISMENE. How have I suffered?
HECUBA. Your husband was at war with –
ISMENE. Why?
HECUBA. – my city. You took pity on us, so he put you in –
ISMENE. A wall. But I didn't die.

HECUBA. No. You'd put on all your jewels. They said you were vain and wanted the dead to honour you in the underworld. O you were clever then! The soldiers waited till their officers had gone. Then they opened your grave. You were sitting up in the dark covered in jewels. They took them and ran away.

ISMENE. They didn't kill me.

HECUBA. Perhaps they were afraid to kill someone they'd found in the tomb.

ISMENE. But I'd lost my mind.

HECUBA. Yes, you were buried for five days. You went into the city and no one recognised you any more. They put us on their ships and sailed for Athens. When the Greeks won the war they thought their troubles were ended. Now they learned they were beginning. The plague came back and spread from ship to ship. The fleet split up. There was a great storm. Many ships sank. I saw the waterspout come out of the grey clouds. It was spinning and shafts of lightning flashed from the sides. It was white and twisting – and ran towards us over the water like a dancer or someone drunk. The sea was flat and white and seething. Then the wall of water hit us. It seized the ship and jerked us inside and half way round the circle and suddenly dropped us out inside, yes, inside the waterspout. It was calm there. The white wall was spinning round us. I looked up and through the top far above I saw the stars. The boat was drifting slowly towards the wall of water on the other side. I don't know how far off it was – yards or miles. When we came near I heard it screaming. I looked over the side of the boat. The sea was flat and smooth, like a sheet pulled down over a bed. As clear as a mirror. I stuck out my hands and saw them chained and roped together in the water. I looked up. The white screaming wall was a foot away. We went into it and shot up to the sky. We came through the top and tobogganed down outside on the slope of water. (*She touches her head in violent pain.*) Ai! This band is tight. The plug's pressing my eye. (*Calm.*) A tree grows, puts out twigs, and people say: See how the tree flourishes! But the twigs grow inside too – and become branches digging deeper and deeper into the soft wood. The tree bears so much fruit it can't all be eaten. Farmers sell it, birds feed their young on it, wasps burrow in it, passers-by sit under the tree and enjoy it. And all the time the branches grow into the tree, and the weight of the arms tightens their roots in the trunk till it's knotted and rimed and the tree stops bearing fruit. Then it's cut down and burned.

ISMENE. How could you see?

HECUBA. I have one eye. But I shall never uncover my eye. Hush! When the storm died down we were wrecked on this island. The fishermen – (*She stops.*)

ISMENE. What is – ?

HECUBA. Sh! A ship!

ISMENE. Hurrah! The merchant – beads and sweets and bright –

HECUBA. No! He comes later! (*Agitated.*) Take me to – (*She starts to walk but stops in agitation.*) No other ship comes to the island!

ISMENE. You frighten me!

HECUBA. No, Ismene, it's nothing. A boat's lost its way.

ISMENE. They're running everywhere!

HECUBA. We've been safe for twelve years. I'd come to rely on it.

GIRLS *run in.*

GEMIL. Ships in the harbour!

ROSSA. Two!

GEMIL. Tied up!

DEMA. No one saw them!

ROSSA. We were all up here!

WOMEN *rush in.*

WOMEN. Stone them!

KALERA (*a woman*). Greeks!

NIMPUS (*a woman*). In the harbour!

WOMEN. Stone them!

NIMPUS. The gods are against them!

GEMIL. Cheats! Cheats!

NIMPUS. And that girl!

KALERA. With our men!

DEMA. Let's stone them!

WOMEN and GIRLS. Stone them!

HECUBA. Be quiet you silly women. The moment something happens you squawk like a gaggle of geese.

DEMA. Stone them!

HECUBA. Who's on the ships? They may be my friends. It'll be nice for you if they come and find my blood on the ground.

KALERA. Throw them in the sea!

ROSSA. Say they died years ago!

NIMPUS. They never came!

HECUBA. And what would your gods do next time the men let down their nets? Wait quietly and see who the strangers are. If they're my enemies they won't harm *you*.

FALGAR (*a woman*). They will!

HECUBA. Bright Apollo
> Who travels each day with the sun

> Let your light show
> Only things fit for the eyes of gods

> Let no foulness stain us
> As you stand on the sea –

> The doorstep of heaven
> That gazes up at the house

The WOMEN *and* GIRLS *move to the right.*

ISMENE (*to* HECUBA). Soldiers.

Slight pause. NESTOR *comes on with* SOLDIERS *and* SAILORS *in working dress. The* VILLAGERS *follow them on.*

NESTOR. Hecuba? Don't be alarmed. I am your friend Nestor.

HECUBA. How did you find me?

NESTOR. It took some time! The sea's so big. We asked the merchants who trade between the islands. In the end we heard of you.

HECUBA. What d'you want?

NESTOR. The Athenian government offers you sanctuary.

HECUBA. Can I go home to Troy?

NESTOR (*sighs*). There is no Troy. Athens has put one of its great new houses at your disposal. The garden's superb! What flowers! What scents! Have you heard of the new Athens? On the hill a great –

HECUBA. I'm a politician's widow: I listen to gossip.

As NESTOR *speaks the* BOYS *return from the race in twos and threes. They join the* VILLAGERS.

NESTOR. Painted palaces and mansions, crowded streets, halls of justice. The public gardens are already mature in our kind Athenian climate. Fruit trees, laurels, olives. Fountains in the squares. Troy was nothing in comparison! And our port – the market of the world! They say one day the doors of our poorest people will hang on silver hinges. You'll have such comfort! Luxury! I remember a famous saying (*Kisses his finger tips.*) mm! our cooks *are* Trojan! New Athens offers peace to its greatest enemy. The world is reconciled. Come and uncover your eye, don't sit here in rancour.

HECUBA. You enjoy your old age, Nestor. So do I.

NESTOR (*shrugs*). Well well, I won't try to change you. I know that's not easy.

HECUBA. What other reason made Athens send me so distinguished a visitor? Come to the point.

NESTOR. Time only heals if you let it.

HECUBA. Your beard must be very long.

NESTOR. It is a bit longer.

HECUBA. And as white as a baby.

NESTOR. Yes, but I have rosy cheeks and my eyes are as bright as when I was young! I feel like a boy! These last few years have been the happiest of my life. We worked like miners to build our new city! We wanted to live to enjoy it! If you looked at me you'd see how prosperous Athens is, ma'am. I've come for the statue.

HECUBA (*laughs*). I'd forgotten the statue!

NESTOR. These good people say you're priestess of their shrine Is the statue here?

HECUBA. The island's poor. You work or you don't eat. This is the most I can do. Ismene sweeps and fetches for me.

NESTOR. Is that Ismene? My god I wouldn't have known. (*To* ISMENE.) Strange, strange, strange. The cleverest woman married to the handsomest man, my dear. Not a wise match.

HECUBA. Nestor I can't give you the statue. I can do much better: tell you it's gone.

NESTOR. Gone?

HECUBA. Yes.

NESTOR. Where?

HECUBA (*points*). There.

NESTOR. The sea?

HECUBA. When our boat was floundering in the storm the captain – a Greek – panicked. We shipped water so I told them to throw it overboard.

NESTOR. . . . I'm confused . . .

HECUBA. We survived, but the captain drowned.

NESTOR (*bewildered*). . . . That would be sacrilege . . .

HECUBA (*shrugs*). O it was long ago. And time heals all.

NESTOR. Heros will be angry. We've searched so long! He can be violent you know. It's hidden on the island!

HECUBA. Surely you're too old to worry about his rages!

NESTOR. I was looking forward to taking it home. All that cheering and waving! – I'm out of breath. The climb from the quay.

HECUBA. Carve a fake.

NESTOR (*after a slight pause*). I'd rather not. I'm too old to meddle in sacred things. Doesn't give the gods time to forget it before you meet them. It's gone, he'll have to accept it – he's mortal like the rest of us. (*Sighs.*) I wonder if he'll take away my new house. I planned the garden to catch the sun.

TEMI. Sir will you eat with us in our hall? We have the best fish.

PORPOISE. And good olives and bread.

TEMI. And the merchant buys our wine for the other islands.

NESTOR. Gladly, gladly. In the old days of my father – my brothers and uncles and I, we often sailed round the islands. Fishing, hunting in the mountains. Saw a lion once. There in front of me on the path! Grrrrraaaaahhhhh! I ran – I was a boy. I slept by the fire on the beach many times and woke up to hear the sea. Will you eat with us?

HECUBA. Me? No, you disturb me – bitter words come in my head. I've no wish for revenge. But I don't want to remember. You'll eat well with them.

NESTOR. As you wish. I'll rest my men for a few days. I'll say goodbye before I go.

HECUBA. Say it now. Spare your legs.

NESTOR. True. Goodbye. Strange. (*To* TEMI.) I need food and water for my ships.

TEMI. You can have what we've got.

NESTOR. Don't expect to be overpaid. (*He wags his finger.*) Athens didn't build big houses by throwing money away.

> NESTOR *and the men go.* ISMENE, *the* WOMEN *and* GIRLS *follow them out.* HECUBA *is alone.*

HECUBA. Ah! Ah! I can hear my grandchild's voice. I thought I'd forgotten. Let me die quietly here, in dignity . . . I love to play on the beach, there's nothing to bump into – O not running and horseplay, losing your breath at my age isn't a pleasure – but walk on the sand and let the water-line guide me. I listen to the sea and it washes away all my anger and so I'm at peace. Now there's a storm blowing up. Millions of drops of rain, each one with a human face.

> O Apollo of the bright hair
> No one can watch your journey
> Over the shining water

Or see those eyes that never weep
But you warm us
And we hear the calls of your children
Who play in the sea

TWO

One month later.
A MAN *stands by the rock. He is deformed, short and has dark hair and pitted skin. He takes some of the latest offering and eats it mechanically. He is not hungry.* HECUBA *comes from the hut. She walks towards the sea, stops, clasps her hands tightly together, and then walks on.*

MAN. Sanctuary.
HECUBA. What?
MAN. I won't hurt you.
HECUBA. Go away! There's no sanctuary on this island. You came with the merchant.
MAN. I stowed away!
HECUBA. A criminal!
MAN. No, I ran from the mines. The merchant let me work my passage. But he'd hand me over when we came to an island with a garrison – for the money.
HECUBA. This is not my island. Speak to the islanders.
MAN. Speak for me. They'd stone me. Let me work here – fetch water – I could farm some land – guard this place.
HECUBA. A place doesn't have to be guarded on this island if it's holy.
MAN. Everywhere we landed I looked out for somewhere safe. Time was running out – we'd get to the big islands soon. Then I heard about this: it was as if god had helped me! If I must die I'll die here in the sun, not in the mine.

ISMENE *hurries on.*

ISMENE. Guess, guess! They sold things cheap in the end. I carried a lady's parcel home and she gave me some money. Feel! (*She puts a little doll in* HECUBA's *hand.*) Blue eyes! And a little dress! (*Suddenly realising, to the* MAN.) The merchant's gone!

MAN (*pointing off*). Look! Fishermen.

ISMENE (*stares angrily from* HECUBA *to the* MAN. *Then she snatches the doll*). My doll! I carried the lady's parcel. (*Presses the doll to her breast.*) I found it on the quay. I couldn't give it back. The ship had gone.

HECUBA. Sh!

ISMENE. My doll! Mine! Mine!

ISMENE *hurries into the hut.* TEMI *and* PORPOISE *come on with* ORVO *behind them.*

TEMI. D'you know this man?

HECUBA. He says he's –

TEMI. The merchant told us. He's run from the mines.

HECUBA. Yes.

PORPOISE. You think you're safe? (*She shakes her head.*) The Greeks were here not long ago.

MAN. I thought it was safe – (*He stops in bewilderment.*)

PORPOISE. At least he's used to hard work.

MAN. Yes let me work! Up here out of your way –

TEMI. No, that's not seemly. Besides, it's women's work. You can work in the boats.

PORPOISE. He'll wish he was still down the mines.

ORVO *laughs.*

TEMI. Did he threaten you?

HECUBA. No.

TEMI (*to* PORPOISE). See what the village says.

PORPOISE *and* ORVO *take the* MAN *out left.*

Will the Greeks come back?

HECUBA. I don't know.

TEMI. Are we safe?

HECUBA. Yes.

TEMI. Some of them want to get in the boats and sail off. The sea's big. There are other islands, perhaps better than this.

HECUBA. You'd always be watching the horizon for the Greeks.

TEMI. That's what I said. But now he's here (*He gestures offstage.*) . . . ? The mines belong to Athens.

HECUBA. If the Athenians come you'll drown him out at sea and say he's never been here. That's how you get rid of criminals and unnatural births. He's at risk, not you.

TEMI. True. I'll go down.

> TEMI *bows and goes.*

THREE

A month later.
ISMENE *sweeps the rocks. The* MAN *comes in.* ISMENE *stops.*

ISMENE. You're not supposed to be here.

MAN. I waited till the old woman went down on the beach.

ISMENE. The fishermen'll catch you.

MAN. Let me watch.

ISMENE. Watch?

MAN (*points*). I often hide over there and watch you.

ISMENE. Why? I'm not beautiful.

MAN. How d'you know?

ISMENE. The women say.

MAN. Ha! They're jealous. They smell of fish.

ISMENE. Jealous of me? I'm a slave!

MAN. So are they – cook, scrub, make nets, gut fish, bear kids.

ISMENE *goes into the hut. The* MAN *looks round and then starts to follow her.*

ISMENE (*off*). Don't go!

The MAN *stops.* ISMENE *comes out of the hut with the doll.*

ISMENE. There! D'you like it?

MAN. O god you're beautiful.

ISMENE. Well. You've watched. Now go away.

MAN. I want you.

ISMENE. Like the fishermen – they quarrel with their wives and then beckon me with their finger!

MAN (*points off*). Come over there.

ISMENE. No.

MAN. Is it the old woman? Does she spy on you with her eye?

ISMENE (*shocked*). No! Does she?

MAN. At her age they're like children! She'll be dead soon. Then what'll you do?

ISMENE. Take over here.

MAN. The women won't let you.

ISMENE. They will!

MAN. They know about you and their men. That's not how priestesses are trained.

ISMENE. Go away! I work hard – do what I'm told – what more can I do?

MAN. I could look after you when she's dead.

ISMENE. What did you have in your mine?

MAN. Silver.

ISMENE. And what's that dirt in your face?

MAN (*shrugs*). Dust from the rock.

He goes to her and holds her.

ISMENE. I can't.

MAN. The hut. Come on. Please.

They go into the hut. Immediately the door shuts HECUBA *comes on. She gropes to the rocks and sits. She wraps herself in a shawl.* ISMENE *comes out of the hut.*

ISMENE (*flustered*). I was asleep – I swept up and then –

HECUBA. I'd have stayed on the beach but the wind's up. I have to be careful at my age. Go back to him.

The MAN *comes from the house and starts to leave.*

HECUBA. Is he there? Stay here – I'll go inside.

The MAN *makes a noise of disgust.*

ISMENE. You're jealous!

HECUBA. Ha! At my age your emotions are simpler. And a lot simpler than wanting to – (*She gestures towards the* MAN.) – thank god. (*To the* MAN.) You – wherever you are – I don't spy, with my good eye or the bad one. (*The* MAN *says nothing.*) The rest was true. If I knew she had a chance to be happy when I was dead, that would be something – not much, fools will still burn cities, but I can't change the whole world. (*The* MAN *doesn't move.*) So you'll look after my daughter? You can't even look after yourself. What'll you do when the Athenians come?

MAN. The villagers said they won't!

HECUBA. They'll come.

MAN. Let them! One slave? They won't even notice!

HECUBA. They tell me you're crooked. That'll give you away.

MAN. I'll hide.

HECUBA. Fool! Hide and seek! The fishermen'll drown you the moment the Greeks come over the horizon. If they didn't kill you the Athenians would. I'm an authority on Greek justice. They have big nets to catch little sprats.

MAN. What shall I do?

HECUBA. I'll tell the fishermen to prove their loyalty by handing you over – and I'll tell the Greeks to let you go. They'll fuss but agree.

MAN. Why?

HECUBA. They're sentimental under the armour. And besides, they want something from me and they think I can be stubborn. You're all I shall ask in return. (*Shrugs.*) I might as well get something out of them.

MAN (*craftily*). And what d'you want out of me?

HECUBA (*suddenly quietly, fiercely angry*). In your mine you were as safe as a mouse in its hole.

MAN. Ha! You haven't been down there.

HECUBA. O you'd have lived a few more years. Rats don't last long once they scuttle out to the light. You searched all the seas for a safe place: and walked into this trap. I'm the only one who can save your life . . . (*Sneer.*) And you ask what I want in return . . .

MAN (*slight silence*). I – I didn't understand. I'm sorry. (*Silence.*) What can I do? I can take care of your daughter.

HECUBA. Like all men! Reasonable now. When he came: (*Mimics.*) 'Huff, huff! O god you're beautiful!' – I've had sons, some of them almost reached your age. You couldn't have said anything reasonable about the weather!

MAN (*to* ISMENE). I'll come to see you tomorrow. I'll take care of you. I'm not much, with this body. But you don't seem to mind. (*He goes to* HECUBA.) The villagers like me. Between us she'll be safe. Some arrangement can be made.

The MAN *takes* HECUBA'*s hand and then starts to go.*

ISMENE. What's an – an arrangement?

HECUBA. Hush . . .

ISMENE *goes away crying.* HECUBA *is alone.*

FOUR

A month later.
A formal meeting. On the left, facing right, HEROS, AIDES, *the* CHIEF ARCHITECT *and* GUARDS. *On the right, facing left,* HECUBA *and a few paces behind her, as her guide,* ORVO. *The other* VILLAGERS *are upstage, left and left centre. Some of them surround* HECUBA. *All the* GREEKS *wear ceremonial military or professional dress.* HEROS *looks like Michelangelo's Lorenzo de' Medici at the Basilica of San Lorenzo.*

HEROS. Queen Hecuba the Athenian state greets you. You have heard of the New Athens. Of the pax athenaea that covers the world. We have replaced fear with reason, violence with law, chaos with order, plunder with work –

HECUBA. I told Nestor the –

HEROS. New Athens has changed the world! Not made it perfect, but a place where it's wise to hope. One day –

HECUBA. The statue's in the sea.

HEROS. Athens! Even the name's a blessing! Athens of marble and silver! It sparkles in the sun and floats like a ship in the moonlight. The people say that soon the doors of our poorest will hang on silver. The temple is marble. The walls of the inner shrine are covered in silver. The great doors are solid silver. The bowls and knives and chains for the sacrifice are silver. The priests carry silver rods. The centre of the shrine is a floor of beaten silver where the goddess will stand. Her simple stone will remind us that the wise are humble.

HECUBA. What will you put in its place?

HEROS. The goddess will stand there.

HECUBA. It's lost.

HEROS. No, she's in the sea, and we shall find her.

HECUBA. But . . . (*Stops.*) In the sea?

HEROS. Nestor says you know where she is. You gave the order to throw her in.

HECUBA. I can't be exact.

HEROS. The sea's shallow round these islands. The fishermen are good sailors. (*The* FISHERMEN *lower their heads and shuffle their feet.*) They'll drag the bottom with nets.

HECUBA. There was a storm.

HEROS. Don't see the statue as lost. It's hidden! The whole world was upside down. That's why the goddess hid in the sea: it's the safest place. (*To the* FISHERMEN.) We'll divide the sea into squares. You'll drag from square to square till it's found.

A ripple of laughter from the VILLAGERS.

HECUBA. That will take time.

HEROS (*shrugs*). We could find it tomorrow. Or today! Remember the goddess of Good Fortune is on our side! (*To the* CHIEF ARCHITECT.) Make a start.

(*The* CHIEF ARCHITECT *goes. The* SOLDIERS *move in on the* VILLAGERS. *One of the* YOUNG MEN *is pushed – a moment's scuffle. The* SOLDIERS *push the* VILLAGERS *out. An* AIDE *nods to* ORVO *to go.* HEROS *gestures to his* AIDES *to go. He is alone with* HECUBA. *He takes off his helmet.*)

How is your life here?

HECUBA. Nestor said you haven't changed.

HEROS (*studies his face in the side of his helmet*). Not too much. (*He gestures after his* AIDES.) I've sent my staff off to the harbour. Come to Athens. Share our good fortune. You say nothing. Nestor told me Ismene lost her mind.

HECUBA. O, she doesn't dribble.

HEROS. When I thought she'd . . . (*He leaves the sentence unfinished.*) I married again.

HEROS *takes* HECUBA *to the rocks. She sits and he stands in front of her.*

So at last you have me in your hands.

HECUBA. O, I'll tell you where to search.

HEROS. I'd hoped to find you more – at peace –

HECUBA. I am.

HEROS. – reconciled. You're strong. You have nothing and want nothing, so you have nothing to lose. Yet you have what I want. No power on earth can move you. I'm in your power. I've never been in this situation before.

HECUBA (*laughs lightly*). It's easy for me to want nothing. How long will you stay?

HEROS. A month, if I have to. Then I must get back to Athens. The search can go on, of course, till it's found. I ought to get it started. Goodbye.

HEROS *goes out.* ISMENE *comes from the hut.*

ISMENE. Was that my husband?

HECUBA. Yes.

ISMENE (*suddenly angry*). I'm a child! A big stupid animal!

HECUBA. Sh!

ISMENE. Sh! Sh! Hush! Hush! Nothing I say matters! I'm an animal who gets two meals a day for being house trained and taking you round on a lead. Hush! You could help me – if you opened your eye!

HECUBA. Open my eye?

ISMENE. I have to tell you everything I see – but I don't know what I see. And now that man and his soldiers nodding and winking! What does that mean? I'm afraid!

HECUBA. No – I've kept my promise too long. I left the world when my children were killed –

ISMENE. You call me daughter!

HECUBA. My real children! I can't go back to the world when –

ISMENE. But the world comes here! That man! Those soldiers –!

HECUBA. No! Let me sit patiently in my darkness. I've earned this happiness –

ISMENE. When I look at your face I see something new. I look at

you and think I'm going to remember. I stare at your face – but
it stays blank! If we looked at each other my mind would come
back!

HECUBA. I smile – isn't that enough?

ISMENE. No! No! You think you smile like the guardian of this
shrine! You look like an old hag grinning at herself in the
mirror! You frighten me more than the Greeks! They put me in
prison but you're my gaoler!

HECUBA. Take me inside! Gaoler? Oh, you get the best of it,
believe me! No, this is stupid – boasting about our sufferings
like two old women fighting for fish! If I uncovered my eye –
I'd have to keep it uncovered, once I'd seen the light! I won't!
The dead are dead, the past is past, my children are gone.
Ismene, don't remind me!

ISMENE. You call me daughter. I don't call you mother. Why call
me daughter? – doesn't that remind you?

HECUBA (*groping towards the hut*). I'm really tired.

ISMENE. Don't call me daughter!

HECUBA. Not if it offends! Now you've hooked a man you show
your true colours. Not that he's much to boast of.

ISMENE. Bitch!

HECUBA (*dismissive*). I've been called that before by a Greek.

ISMENE. Bitch!

HECUBA. My little joke. You know your mind's weak, Ismene.
You don't understand jokes unless we explain them to –

ISMENE. You bitch!

HECUBA. Perhaps. Am I?

ISMENE. O you are!

HECUBA. We've never quarrelled before. Now we're screaming
like fishwives. Once I thought I would open my eye . . . I
imagined the scene. Some great occasion. I looked, and recognised a child left on the mountain. Or reconciled two brothers.
I'm not a bitch. You mustn't call me a bitch.

ISMENE. I told you I'm afraid. I can't lead you any more.

HECUBA. If I were a priestess a god would come down now and

tell me what to do. Instead, my enemies come – and I must be ready again. Yes, ready for all my old anger to sweep through me, like the fire in Troy. Help me to take it off.

ISMENE. Yes, yes.

ISMENE *helps* HECUBA *to unfasten the bands from the eye-plug.*

HECUBA. Gently.

ISMENE. Gently.

HECUBA. Careful (*The cover is removed.*) I'll keep my eye shut. Shut – then slowly – with my back to the sun! Then cover it!

ISMENE. Gently.

HECUBA. Give me your hand.

HECUBA *holds* ISMENE's *hand in one hand and shades her eyes with the other. Slowly she opens her eye a little.* ISMENE *peers closer.*

ISMENE. O I can see your poor eye . . . A white line under the red – . . .

HECUBA. Ismene . . .

ISMENE. A thin white line . . . like the moon . . . under the red –. What can you see? Look, my hand. (*She holds her hand in front of* HECUBA's *face.*)

HECUBA. Ismene . . . a light.

ISMENE. What?

HECUBA. A light! A light! (ISMENE *steps back.*) The plug! My band!

HECUBA *whimpers, covers her eye with one hand and gropes for the band on the rock with the other.*

Ismene, are you there?

ISMENE (*pushing the band into* HECUBA's *hand*). Yes!

HECUBA (*covering her face*). A light!

ISMENE *runs into the hut.* HECUBA *sits alone on the rock. She tries to calm herself.*

(*Quietly.*) A light . . . Apollo . . .

ISMENE *runs from the house with a light.*

ISMENE. Here!

HECUBA. Is it here?

ISMENE. Yes!

HECUBA (*uncovers her eye*). Where? Where? Is it lit?

ISMENE. Lit. Lit. (*She holds the light closer to* HECUBA's *face.* HECUBA *reaches for it and pulls it closer.*) Too close! What d'you see, my darling?

HECUBA. Nothing.

ISMENE. Look!

HECUBA. I am.

ISMENE. Careful! Too close!

HECUBA. There's nothing.

ISMENE. I'll wash it! (*She turns to go.*) Water!

HECUBA. Nothing!

ISMENE. There will be. It's dirt. (*She wipes at* HECUBA's *eye with the binding.*) Close it!

HECUBA. I'm blind!

ISMENE. In time – in time –

HECUBA. There's nothing!

ISMENE. There must be!

HECUBA. No light. Not even a shadow. Nothing!

ISMENE. O Hecuba we uncovered it too quickly. Stupid, stupid. We've lost your sight. We should have done it in the house.

HECUBA. No, nothing. No glimmer – not even a moment. It was covered so long – injured, diseased – the sight went long ago. I've been blind for years and didn't know it. I thought I could choose! O Ismene that day has come back! (*She stops.*) My child, my child – you? You saw my eye. Did you remember?

ISMENE. No.

HECUBA. Nothing? Nothing for both of us?

ISMENE. We couldn't look at each other.

HECUBA. No. (*Slight pause.*) I wounded myself too deeply. I jabbed round with the knife. I had no chance. But you – perhaps you'll start to remember.

ISMENE. I don't know.

HECUBA. I'll never be angry with you again Ismene. Perhaps you shall understand. Oh my child, my child – the child I haven't lost. You love me. And look, a blind old woman covered in tears because she loves her daughter.

ISMENE *leads* HECUBA *into the house.*

FIVE

A month later.
HECUBA *and the* MAN.

MAN. They catch netfulls of fish and tip them back in the sea. If fish could think they'd say men were mad. How long will he search?

HECUBA. Sh . . .

MAN. He promised a lot of money to the crew that found it. The fishermen were excited – now they don't care. They grin at each other while they work. He puts soldiers into every boat to make sure they work properly. What do soldiers know about fishing? They keep shouting orders that don't mean anything. The nets aren't even tight. If it *was* there he couldn't find it!

HECUBA (*sits on the bench in front of the house*). The villagers are afraid. They go through the movements pretending to fish, like mad people working with nothing.

HEROS *comes on from the beach, upstage. He wears a short tunic but no helmet or armour. He carries a sword in a scabbard at his belt. The* MAN *moves away downstage left.*

HEROS. I walked on the beach. I haven't been so alone for years. In Athens I move in procession. Bump into guards. I'd like to stay.

HECUBA. The month's gone.

HEROS. A few more days. A week. A thought keeps coming in my head. It's so clear. Perhaps we've already found it – on the first day – one of our nets scraped it up from the bottom – and then it slipped back. I see it so clearly: falling back in the water. Then slowly rocking, backwards and forwards. (*Calmly and thoughtfully.*) Perhaps we shouldn't move on to new areas. Go back over the old ones. (*Sits on the ground.*) Is this your runaway?

HECUBA. Yes.

HEROS. The law is: you're taken back to the mine and killed under ground in front of your fellows. No exceptions. But I've been asked for mercy, and as this island is half outside the world, I allow it. Keep out of the soldiers' way.

The MAN *falls to the ground. He cries.*

HEROS (*looks round*). Quiet as sleep. They call you the bitch of Asia – a whole continent trails after your name like a comet. I have only a city. But a great one.

HECUBA. The currents may have carried it away.

HEROS. Not far. Too heavy. The fishermen know where to look.

HECUBA. Sand's drifted over it.

HEROS. The bottom's quite firm.

HECUBA. If it's heavy, it fell down a crevasse. What will you do if you can't find it?

HEROS. One day I'll look over the side of the boat and see it smiling up at me from the bottom.

HECUBA. But if you don't?

HEROS. It's not to make me famous. It's a millstone round my neck. God rot it. I must close the past! Say: finished. Not all that rational. But you cover your eye. That's not rational. I look at the face that Priam kissed – and it's a mask. If I could see your eye I'd know if you lied.

HECUBA. No, you'd search for some other sign.

HEROS. I questioned the sailors who were in the boat with you. One even helped to throw her out. Imagine! – she was in the hands of that little wizened man. You're the only one who took a bearing on the rocks. (*He sits by* HECUBA *on the bench.*) Have you told me the truth, Hecuba?

HECUBA. Yes.

HEROS. But why? I'm your enemy. I killed your family, destroyed your home –. Of course I was raving with war-madness, but I did it.

HECUBA. There are some things I thank you for. You got rid of the statue.

HEROS. No, you still have it. Out in the sea. You sit here and listen to the water. All day. Does it tell you what we do? Laugh at us? Quietly tell you where the goddess is?

HECUBA (*stands*). Well, I've done what I can to help.

HEROS. One day they'll bring her out in a net. The net will be full of slippery seaweed and fish threshing for life. It'll stretch and bulge as if she was alive inside. Then – I reach out and help her to step from the net. Is my wife in there? (*He points to the hut.*) I want to speak to her.

HECUBA. She may not want to speak to you.

HEROS. I'll tell her about the past. That could cure her.

MAN (*to* HECUBA). It'll make her worse.

HECUBA. Hush! Who said you could interrupt? (*Thinks, then speaks to* HEROS.) Yes. But be careful.

HEROS. O, I'll handle it.

HECUBA (*to the* MAN). Fetch her out.

HEROS. No, let him take you down to the beach.

The MAN *starts to lead* HECUBA *out.*

HECUBA. If she remembers . . . be patient.

HEROS. I'll shout when I'm finished.

The MAN *and* HECUBA *go out upstage right.* HEROS *waits till they've gone. Then he taps on the door and steps back. After a moment* ISMENE *comes out.*

ISMENE. O. You want the old lady? She's on the –
HEROS. Who am I?
ISMENE. A Greek.
HEROS. A rich man. What shall I give you?
ISMENE. O . . . you Greeks are silly.
HEROS. Are we?
ISMENE. Looking for a stone in the sea! You won't find it.
HEROS. Why not?
ISMENE. Even if you looked the day after it was lost, it would have been swept away.
HEROS. You were in the boat when it was lost. You remember the storm?
ISMENE. There're always storms.
HEROS. Troy? You went round and round the walls shouting peace!
ISMENE (*indifferently*). I don't remember.
HEROS. Shut your eyes.
ISMENE. Have you brought me something?
HEROS. Hm-hmm.
ISMENE. No, I'm not a child today.
HEROS. Shut your eyes.
ISMENE. O! But be quick!

ISMENE *squeezes her eyes shut.* HEROS *puts his hand on her breast. She opens her eyes and runs upstage.*

HEROS. Stop!
ISMENE (*faces him*). What d'you want?
HEROS. Where's the statue? Tell me! *Please!*
ISMENE. I told you I can't!
HEROS. Try!

ISMENE *saunters away, stops, then faces him again.*

ISMENE. I know you're my husband, you know.

HEROS. You remember?

ISMENE. I peeped the first time you came and asked Hecuba.

HEROS. Sleep with me tonight.

ISMENE. Tch tch tch.

HEROS. I'm said to be handsome.

ISMENE. Beauty doesn't attract me any more. That went too.

HEROS (*takes out coins*). I'll pay.

ISMENE. For a doll? They cost a lot!

HEROS (*suddenly quietly very angry*). Ismene, in war the good hides behind the bad. You're the only one I've seen stay innocent through a war: I had to stop that – the bad was hiding behind the good. I raised my sword. But there was no malice. It was for Athens. Will you forgive me?

ISMENE (*sits and plays in the sand, running it through her fingers*). I do.

HEROS (*still seething with quiet anger*). A leader really needs only one virtue – restraint – but many vices. A good ruler knows how to hate. He even knows the limits of restraint. From time to time he surrenders it to anger. How else can he make the people afraid?

ISMENE (*building a sand castle*). Here's the drawbridge.

HEROS. From time to time the people must be afraid – not of him but of each other – or the city falls apart. Fear is like a seed which he plants at the top of the tree.

ISMENE. Here's the door.

HEROS. I'm taking you back to Athens.

ISMENE. No! No!

HEROS. Don't be afraid.

ISMENE. I am! I am!

HEROS. Of me?

ISMENE. Of *me*! I won't go! I can't behave – look at me now! (*She throws down the sand.*) They'd lock me away in a city!

HEROS. My child, Athens can give you a prison bigger than the whole of this island! We're that rich!

ISMENE. But the sea's not a wall!

HEROS. Then think of what I've said. If I can't find the statue I must prove – to the citizens of Athens – that I made every effort to find it. In effect that would mean the painful destruction of these islanders and the razing of their village. I have a duty to Athens not to let chance make me a laughing stock. I take a duty to Athens very seriously: it is the home of freedom. I put myself in this worst possible light so you understand my position. I shall plant the seed on top of the tree. Unless you remember.

ISMENE. These people aren't to blame!

HEROS. I've always wanted peace, and everyone to be happy when they can. Yet they'll be killed to satisfy people who don't even know their names.

ISMENE. Don't hurt them! Please!

HEROS. When the wind blows the apples fall – or the tree gets too heavy and the wind blows that down.

ISMENE. Yes – now – I remember –

HEROS. What?

ISMENE. The war – and the storm – at sea – that was terrible! – and – where the ship was sunk?

HEROS. I tried to help.

ISMENE. I do remember! Round and round the wall shouting peace!

HEROS. Liar.

ISMENE. I do! I do! She tells the truth anyway! Why don't you believe her? (*Cries.*) Don't hurt them!

HEROS. You mustn't cry. (*He gives her the coins.*) There. You've been very good.

ISMENE. Really?

HEROS. Yes. No tears. (*He goes upstage and calls.*) Hecuba! (*He comes back to* ISMENE.) Excuse me. I must go.

> HEROS *goes out.* ISMENE *goes upstage and meets the* MAN *coming on.*

MAN. You've been crying! You remembered!

ISMENE. No. Nothing. He said –

MAN. Then you can stay? Yow-eee! (*He tickles her.*) What an idiot! Typical woman! Mind like a hole with a gap in it! No manners! Can't behave!

ISMENE (*laughing and struggling*). Who can't walk straight? Who's got a dirty face!

MAN (*tickling her*). Say sorry!

ISMENE (*laughing*). I'm not! I'm not! I'm not!

MAN (*tickling her*). I'll give you something to be sorry for.

HECUBA *is coming slowly on stage.*

ISMENE. Make him stop!

HECUBA. What's he doing?

ISMENE. Hurting me! (*Laughing.*) I'm sorry!

MAN (*tickling her*). Not enough!

ISMENE. O stop! Stop! Stop!

HECUBA. Hush! Children! Behave yourselves! We'll scandalize the village –! (*The* MAN *starts tickling her.*) Stop it! (*She laughs.*) Ismene make him stop! O dear. (*Laughs.*) We'll scandalize the –

ISMENE. I'm not sorry! I'm not sorry!

The MAN *chases* ISMENE.

Pig!

HECUBA. Stop it! The pair of you!

MAN. Mind like the handle of a bucket and nothing underneath!

They calm down.

HECUBA. Tickling a woman of my age! Well – you didn't remember! What did he say?

ISMENE. I've forgotten that too! It's his fault!

MAN *and* HECUBA *laugh.*

MAN. Did he scare you?

ISMENE. I forget!

They laugh.

HECUBA. Well – go indoors.

ISMENE. You see! She treats me like a child.

HECUBA. I want to *talk* to him – not listen to your chatter. (*To the* MAN.) Tell her. She might listen to you.

ISMENE. If he's staying I'm going anyway.

ISMENE *goes into the house.*

HECUBA. He won't find his stone. So he'll kill the islanders for a vote in Athens.

MAN. I ran over half a continent to get here. I won't sit down while he sharpens his knives.

HECUBA. Sh! It was clear when that smiling old man came and said 'statue' that one day this island would be pulled out of the sea by its roots and the people on it shaken down like ants. He should be killed. But if the islanders kill him to save their lives, his soldiers will kill them. Absurd! He must be killed! I've walked on the beach and daydreamed of killing him myself. Sheer fantasy! I'm blind and I haven't strength to scratch him with a pin. He'd chop *you* down like a stick. Yet he must be killed!

MAN. I'll take my chance.

HECUBA. Huh! We need more than that. Tell me about your mine.

TWO SOLDIERS *and a* SERGEANT *come on.*

MAN. Soldiers.

SERGEANT. Don't be alarmed.

HECUBA. What d'you want?

SERGEANT. Protect you from the villagers.

HECUBA. The pax Athenaea has reached the island.

HECUBA *stands and the* MAN *leads her towards the hut.*

(*To the* MAN.) Come in.

SIX

Three months later.
Day, overcast. NESTOR *stands by the hut.* HECUBA *is inside. The*
door is open. The MAN *sits and watches the beach.* TWO SOLDIERS
lounge upstage – only one of them has been seen at the end of Scene
Five.

NESTOR. The storm season's started. If he doesn't leave now the
journey will be dangerous. He took up power – and uses it to
sit on an island and look for a pin in the ocean! Ha! A soldier's
place is his post. Waiting on the wind and sea – that's not the
soldiering I understand.

HECUBA (*off*). He sat outside Troy for five years.

NESTOR. The Athenians don't even want his statue. O, they'd
call it a sign from heaven – but they've ignored plenty of *them*
in the past!

HECUBA (*off*). He's still on the beach?

MAN. Yes.

NESTOR (*goes to look*). Up and down, staring at the sea. I'd better
get it over. (*He calls and waves.*) Yoo-hoooooo!

MAN. He's running.

HECUBA (off). He thinks you've found it. But he won't run too
fast. Then he needn't feel ashamed if he has to hide his
disappointment.

NESTOR. He could sit on this island for the rest of his life. Talk
and drink, not bother to wash his beard for weeks on end. I've
seen it happen. Go out with one fisherman and a boat now and
then. Study the currents so he thinks he only needs to go out
one day a year as long as it's the right one. And when he's old
someone will take him to Athens and he won't recognise the
place he built! Then come back here for the last time and fish
for it with a rod and bent pin.

HECUBA (*off*). But before he becomes a quiet little man peacefully angling in a boat, he'll turn the world upside down with an axe.

NESTOR (*quietly to himself, as he watches* HEROS *on the beach*). My poor boy, I wish I brought you good news!

> HEROS *comes on.* NESTOR *goes towards him with open arms – but* HEROS *stops some way off.*

NESTOR (*expansively*). My boy . . .

HEROS. Nestor, what are you doing here?

NESTOR. The council sent me.

HEROS (*coming downstage. Trying to control his breath*). Phew! Watching the sea change colour. Doesn't sparkle this time of year. Grey. Like dirty windows. (*To* NESTOR, *pointing down at the ground.*) I meant *here*! (*To the* SOLDIERS.) Your orders were: let no one come.

FIRST SOLDIER. Sir . . .

HEROS. No one!

NESTOR. O, they know me of old – I'm an officer –

HEROS. I said no one, Nestor.

NESTOR. Then make your orders clear. So we know where we stand.

HEROS. I was clear: no one.

NESTOR. My mistake.

HEROS. Report to your officer after duty.

FIRST and SECOND SOLDIERS. Sir.

HEROS (*to* NESTOR). You think I'm unreasonable. This place is almost part of the sea. We *feel* it. All except you. Would you rush into a temple and yoo-hoo? I risk the welfare of Athens being here. It's our duty to take absolute care. We owe it to Athens. Yoo-hooo! (*Distant roll of thunder.*) It's a matter of military discipline. (*Flatly.*) Now thunder.

NESTOR. I'm surprised I'm not accused of farting.

HEROS. Nestor. Keep the circus for your soldiers. Look, I explain this not to justify myself but out of respect for your age.

NESTOR. The matter's closed. I'm not offended, my boy.

> *A distant roll of thunder.*

HEROS (*quietly, angrily*). Yoo-hoo. (*Calmer.*) Welcome to the island, Nestor. This storm will hold up the search. A day lost now – (*He stops in frustration. Calmer again.*) How is Athens?

NESTOR. Not well. Rebuilding the city has broken down the old ways. Our property – even our lives – need protecting. Ajax and Thersites quarrel through every council. It's embarrassing. They hold meetings behind everyone's back. We need you, my son, not the statue.

HECUBA (*off*). An empty temple would have great dignity. We should worship the force, not the image.

HEROS. I've seen cats piddling against empty temples.

NESTOR. The council orders you to sail within a week. They give clear orders too.

HECUBA (*off*). I'll fetch a bowl of water from the sea. Place that in the temple. The Athenians would understand that.

HEROS. Yet it might be tomorrow. Even while we're talking they may have found it. (*A distant roll of thunder.*) It may be standing on the quay. Unless the fishermen have hidden it to extort more money.

NESTOR. The winter storms are starting. We must get away.

HEROS. I'll search the village. If I put them under canvas they'll be easier to watch. To go away now! We might have stopped within an inch – one inch of sand – and tomorrow it would have been ours! I won't stop now!

HECUBA *comes from the hut.*

HECUBA. No. I've had a dream for five nights: so I must believe it. Not in the early morning, like other dreams, but in the middle of the night – as if it came from under the sea.

HEROS. What dream?

HECUBA. The goddess. She tells me she's ready to leave the sea.

HEROS. Yes.

HECUBA. She'll send a sign to the man who will find her. This time the sign will be clear. The man will win a race.

HEROS. An ordinary race?

HECUBA. A foot race round the island.

HEROS. I challenge any man to this race! Greek or Islander!

HECUBA. The goddess has chosen the runners. There are two.

HEROS. I'm one?

HECUBA. Yes.

HEROS. Who's the other?

HECUBA (*gestures around for the* MAN. *He limps to her.*) Him.

HEROS. He's crippled.

HECUBA. You needn't run.

NESTOR. I'm against this. This search for holiness is impious! Do what you have to do and let others judge! Call god when you finish – not when you start!

HECUBA. I dreamed five times.

HEROS. And I'll get the statue? (*No answer.*) It's a trick.

NESTOR. Good! Now we'll get on our ships and go. We have homes, families, money, work. Why why why d'you want more?

The stage is lit by a flash of lightning.

HEROS. She's trying to tell me something. I can't understand. To win I'd risk everything – gladly! But race with a cripple – what do I *risk*? I'm tripped? Lose my way?

A roll of thunder, a little closer.

HECUBA. You can see the whole coast path from the hill in the middle of the island. (*Shrugs.*) You can't lose your way.

HEROS. I'll break my leg!

HECUBA. The path's smooth.

HEROS. No! No! I won't do it!

HECUBA. There is one condition.

HEROS. What?

HECUBA. A prize for the loser. The loser is killed. That's the risk.

NESTOR. I forbid this race. I'll arrest you as mad, Heros! (*To the* SOLDIERS – *indicating the* MAN.) Take him! (*The* SOLDIERS *take hold of the* MAN.)

HEROS. Wait! I begin to see!

HECUBA. You've been given so much: armies, victories, a city, your looks. Now you're offered the greatest gift. But to get that you must hold on to nothing. Be willing to lose – and be content. A small risk. She'll share the small risk with you. If you don't take it – perhaps you'll lose everything.

The MAN *stands between the* TWO SOLDIERS. HEROS *looks at him.*

HEROS. Who are you?

MAN (*shrugs*). I've never been asked before. I don't know. I was born in the mine. In the compound on top. Most are born under. I've heard my mother was a cook. I suppose my father was a guard.

HEROS. That's why the goddess made me save your life: for this!

MAN. When you built your new city our hell grew with it. It's not true the guilty go to hell: only the weak.

HEROS. Enemies of the state or criminals!

MAN (*shakes his head*). I was born there. Why d'you cover your new city in silver? Your mud bricks, the soles of your shoes, are worth more than silver. I know what value is. I made your statues in Athens. You think I'm the broken bits that were chipped away! No – I made their smile.

HEROS. I see why the goddess challenged you! Will you take the risk?

MAN. The work's shaped round our lives as naturally as the seasons. At five I dragged baskets of rock through the tunnels. The rope round my waist cut a groove in my flesh. I was glad when the groove was cut. I was a machine with a gulley – here – for the rope. *That* pain would be kept *there*. An iron cable and a a pulley are oiled where they rub together. The gulley in the flesh can't be oiled. The flesh would go soft. The rope would tear it. It must be two stones. Rubbing together. The flesh of a child. Each day. All day! When the child – with his nipped-in waist like an ant – can lift an axe – he's sent to the face. First we break it with fire. Then we crawl in while it's hot – Athens is built fast! Our hands and knees are hoofs! We don't dig in a straight line. We follow the bend of the seams. They're put there by the devil. Our bodies are twisted round his finger in the dark. Like string. When we're too old to dig we go to the top – corpses surfacing! Old men and women – the difference went long ago, their sex is small knots on the skin – empty the children's baskets and crouch by the trough, sorting and sorting, their hands going up and down, sorting, like the legs of a beetle turned on its back.

HEROS. I didn't make the world.

MAN. Only Athens!

HEROS. Things change. Step by step. Let them out, they'd starve!

MAN. You don't want them to dirty your new streets!

HEROS (*offers his hand*). If I win this race – and every chance says I'll win – then I'll do what I can to help those people.

MAN (*refusing his hand*). You'll go away and forget. Every second of my life – till I ran – was watched by people like you – holding a whip with a silver handle. If you could count our crumbs, you would.

HECUBA. Tomorrow is the feast day. Nestor, you judge the winner. No swords, the day is holy and must not be polluted. (*A distant roll of thunder.*) For this, since it's the last day of the war that destroyed my city, I'll uncover my eye and watch the race from the hill. Go and prepare for tomorrow. Nothing can be done till then.

They go.

SEVEN

The same night.
A violent storm approaches from the sea. The edge of the rain clouds has already reached the island: a few heavy raindrops. Out at sea, lightning and the roar of wind, water, thunder and rain. The MAN *sits motionless, facing the sea.* HECUBA *comes from the hut.*

HECUBA. What can you see?

MAN. The storm hasn't reached us yet.

HECUBA (*comes closer to him*). Be my eyes.

MAN. The sea's rising. The water's black. Tomorrow.

HECUBA. Is there a moon?

MAN. Yes.

HECUBA. And fast clouds!

MAN. Tomorrow!

HECUBA. It's a mad woman with a lamp. Running from window to window.

MAN. I can't run like him.

HECUBA. Run as fast as you can. Then walk straight home and get your sword. Tell me. The lightning!

MAN. Showers of sparks where it hits the water. It lights up the whole sea.

HECUBA (*holds him*). And the serpents?

MAN. There are no serpents.

HECUBA. Yes, yes, where the wind lifts the water in coils.

MAN. Hecuba, go indoors.

HECUBA. Not real serpents, you silly man! Is there a spout?

MAN. What?

HECUBA. A waterspout?

MAN. No.

HECUBA. Ah! But there will be. Tomorrow. Soon. It comes over the edge of the horizon like the finger of a giant. Hauling himself on to the earth. Don't be afraid! When it's gone you see: it's only a bunch of grey hairs in a comb. (*She holds him and strokes his hair.*) I wish you were my grandson.

MAN. Will I die tomorrow?

HECUBA. The spout won't hit us. It crosses down on the rocks. But the whole earth shakes.

MAN. Go into the house.

    HECUBA *walks away from him. The storm is closer.*

(*Calls.*) Ismene!

    ISMENE *comes from the hut.*

ISMENE. Come inside.

MAN. Hecuba's on the beach!

    The storm hits the island.

(*Calls.*) Hecuba! Ismene, we must get her!

ISMENE. She goes out in the storm! She hides in the rocks! She knows where!

MAN. Is she safe?

ISMENE. Quickly!

    ISMENE *and the* MAN *go into the hut.*

EIGHT

The next day.
Afternoon. Still overcast. A bench has been put upstage for NESTOR.
He sits on it with his lap covered by a blanket. SOLDIERS. GIRLS
and OLDER VILLAGERS – *they shout encouragement to runners off stage.*

OLDER VILLAGERS and GIRLS. Yes! Yes! Orvo! Dario! Faster!
Look out! He's catching up! Hyspos! Orvo my love!

The YOUNG MEN *run on to the stage in a close finish.* HYSPOS *wins.*

Hyspos!

The GIRLS *garland all the* BOYS. HYSPOS's *family gather round him.*

HYSPOS'S MOTHER. All the women will envy me in the market!
HYSPOS'S GRANDFATHER. So fast!
HYSPOS (*embracing his grandfather*). It's easy just from the harbour!
HYSPOS'S FATHER. See how well our boy treats the old people!
ALIOS. Let's go up the hill and watch the big race!
GIRLS. No! Our turn! Dance!

The GIRLS *dance, imitating the wind.*

GIRLS. Wheeeeeeeeee!
BOYS (*imitating thunder*).
              Boom! Boom! Boom!
              Sea rocks the boat
              Big man's cradle
GIRLS. Wheeeeeeeeee!
BOYS (*sing*). Boom! Boom! Boom!
              Wind blows wheeeee!
              God panting on his woman

              Crack bang! Crack bang!
              Old man thunder
              Broke his walking stick
              And fell down in the sea!
GIRLS. Wheeeeeeee!

The dance ends. The MAN *has come on.*

NESTOR. Well, here's one fool given up.
ROSSA. Towel and water in the hut.

The MAN *goes into the hut.* SOLDIERS *follow and guard the door.*

NESTOR. Interesting that – the girls' dance. Brr! Hope this farce ends soon. (*Claps his hands.*) Dance! I'm cold!

ORVO (*explaining*). The dance is over for the year. We can't dance it twice.

NESTOR. Dance something else!

ALIOS. That's the winter dance!

ORVO. If we danced something else we wouldn't catch fish!

HYSPOS'S GRANDFATHER. And the moon would stay on her back.

The GIRLS *laugh.*

NESTOR. Peasants . . . ! And me! I sit here and wait for a runner to win a race he's already won because I've disqualified the only other runner. Greek wisdom. (*To* SOLDIERS.) You men take your orders from me today. When our commander gets back he'll be – winded. I'll manage this. (*The* SOLDIERS *look at each other uneasily. To the* FIRST OFFICER.) Don't just stand there! See what's happening!

The FIRST OFFICER *goes to the side of the stage, peers off, then walks off.*

(*To the* SECOND OFFICER.) You! Go and tell my cook. Get my dinner on. And make sure we're ready to go.

The SECOND OFFICER *goes out. The* FIRST OFFICER *comes back.*

FIRST OFFICER. The old woman's coming down the hill.

NESTOR (*holds out his hand*). Rain. A few drops. Huh! I said when I got up: feast day – rain. (*He shouts to* VILLAGERS.) You start working for your living tomorrow! No more playing silly buggers and getting paid fortunes. You women back to gutting the fish! Up to your titties in salt! (*To himself.*) Athens! How I long for my city! I shan't leave again. Past soldiering!

HEROS *dashes in. He collapses, exhausted.* NESTOR *leads the* SOLDIERS *in cheering.*

NESTOR and SOLDIERS. Rah rah hoorah! Rah rah hoorah! Rah rah hoorah!

HEROS. Done! Nestor the statue's ours. Put out – one boat! My god I think she'll walk out – of the sea to us.

NESTOR. The cripple gave up.

HEROS. Where is he?

NESTOR (*points*). Hanging himself in the hut.

The SOLDIERS *guarding the hut, and some* FISHERMEN, *go inside.*

HEROS. Give me that. (*He takes* NESTOR's *blanket and covers himself.*)

NESTOR (*rubbing his hands for warmth*). Have they remembered to pick my olives? I left instructions.

HEROS. I'll stop shivering now. If he had a wife or child – I'd take them in care.

The MAN *comes out of the hut. The group of* SOLDIERS *and* FISHERMEN *follows him. He wears clean clothes and a sword hung in a scabbard.*

HEROS. You'll be killed quickly and given proper burial.

MAN. I won.

HEROS. You're claiming you won?

MAN. I was here first.

JEROS. But you didn't run the race!

MAN. The race was seen.

HEROS. If anyone says you ran the race and were here before me –

NESTOR. Tchaw! Disqualified!

HEROS. – then I was tricked.

NESTOR. Let's end this farce. There's no joy in executions once you're past sixty. Last one I went to caught a cold. But this runaway slave – this public nuisance – should be executed Here. Now.

HEROS. No – I shan't be tricked into cheating! Is that the catch? I cheat and I'm disqualified? Let's see – we don't know she's in this. If this is a conspiracy, who will it take in? It took me an hour to get round this island. He'd hardly get past the harbour by then!

NESTOR. I've given you so much good advice. What good does it do you? I follow you like a faithful mongrel and bark. I should run away. That's what the good people did in the old days – ran away from the lost! (*He draws his sword.*) How ridiculous! An old man waving his sword! Tangled up in my beard! What else can I do?

HEROS. Put that away!

NESTOR. No! No! No! No! No!

HEROS. We'll lose everything! (*He struggles with* NESTOR *for the sword.*) By god put it away! (*He gets the sword and throws it away upstage, onto the beach.*) All of you – no swords! I've come so far I won't be stopped now! I order you! (*To the* SOLDIERS, *indicating* NESTOR.) Arrest him! (*The* SOLDIERS *guard* NESTOR.) I'm on the edge of everything I asked for. I will not have my way barred by your swords. Throw them away! All of you! Down on the beach! (*The* SOLDIERS *throw their swords away upstage.* HEROS *points at the* MAN.) Him too! (*A* SOLDIER *takes the* MAN's *sword and throws it down on the beach. Calls.*) Hecuba! Hecuba! Hecuba! (*To the others.*) We shall tell the truth now. I feel it. At this moment – at last – for once – I cannot lose. The truth speaks for me. Hecuba! I don't administer justice now. It shouts my name!

NESTOR *sits on the bench, guarded by* SOLDIERS, *and cries.*

NESTOR. My son, to whistle up the curs that will devour you.

HECUBA *comes on with* ISMENE. HECUBA's *eyes are uncovered.* ISMENE *stops and lets* HECUBA *walk forward alone.*

HECUBA. Still impatient. I heard you calling. I didn't hurry. How I enjoy these trees! And the clouds. I'd forgotten how strange! The sea's lost – so far out there . . . Look, a ladybird. (*She examines her hand.*) Nine beauty spots. Hard little wings. Scissors! My hand smells. How bitter! A prison. (*She blows the ladybird away.*)

>Fly away fly away fly away home
>Your coat is on fire
>Fly home soon.

HEROS. Did you watch the race while you were admiring the wonders of the world?

HECUBA. Why sneer? There are many beautiful things. I'm sorry I've seen so little of them.

HEROS. You saw the race?

HECUBA. I saw two runners start, and I saw the crippled one win.

HEROS. So you're going to cheat.

HECUBA. Your statue decided this race. Not me.

HEROS. You still go on with it?

HECUBA. I saw you sitting under a tree and smile.

HEROS. Liar! I ran the race! I said you don't have to show who runs the fastest! Walk over the island! But I ran the race! For the goddess's sake! (*He points at* HECUBA.) I trusted this bitch!

HECUBA. You sat under a tree and smiled.

HEROS. Liar!

HECUBA. You stopped. I walked down the hill. You were sitting under the tree like a schoolboy. I stood in front of you and stared at your face. You smiled. You didn't blink. A fly walked across your mouth and over your teeth. The goddess had trapped you under the tree. I shuddered. If I could run I'd have run up the hill. When I got to the top Ismene was still asleep. I'd come from one child to another. I looked back and saw you jump up and run on. You knew nothing of what had happened to you.

HEROS. Good! There was a time when you were not on top of the mountain? Who saw that? Nestor?

NESTOR. My eyes . . .

HEROS (*to* VILLAGERS). You?

PORPOISE. The boys race . . .

TEMI. We were watching . . .

HEROS (*to* HYSPOS's GRANDFATHER). You?

HYSPOS's GRANDFATHER. . . . . Our grandson won . . .

HEROS (*to* SOLDIERS). You? (*The* SOLDIERS *stare uneasily at* NESTOR.) How – how – tell me how this lame man could run round this island in half an hour?

HECUBA. How could you sit and smile under a tree while your life was thrown away? I can't answer your questions. Ask your goddess.

HEROS. I would! Everything! But she's not in my hands! I'd ask the sea if I could!

HECUBA (*to the* MAN). This is your only chance.

MAN. I take it!

> *The* MAN *takes a sword from* HECUBA *and hits* HEROS.

HEROS. Ah no! (*He falls dead.*)

NESTOR. Swords!

HECUBA. Wait! Nestor! Remember Troy! (*General hesitation.*) The cost! I told him: Go! You told him! We begged! Nothing could move him! What did he want? Look! (*She points to the sea. They all turn to face it.*) A little stone in the sea . . . Is it a wonder he's dead?

> *They turn to face* HECUBA.

NESTOR. Did you have that dream?

HECUBA. Yes! A thousand times. Did I invent it? I don't know. Her voice was like the buzzing of thousands of flies. I saw him once giving orders by a heap of bodies outside Troy. Flies buzzed round his mouth. Or perhaps I fell asleep on the hill this afternoon and a fly walked over my nose – and I dreamed it all before I woke up. We drop off all the time at our age, Nestor. Ismene. (ISMENE *covers Hecuba's eyes.*) Now, you want my life? It matters less than nothing to me.

NESTOR. You, no. (*He points to the* MAN.) But him – he walked across this island and brazenly lied to my face!

HECUBA. There was one winner and one loser. One is dead. Don't disturb it.

NESTOR. But I say to myself, shouldn't I ask what is justice? There's too much truth in this story. I can't find the loose ends.

HECUBA. That should only worry the hangman. Take him to the beach and burn him quickly. The storm's coming up. Nestor, get home before the bad weather sets in. You know how to explain this to the Greeks. They'll soon forget him.

SOLDIERS *take* HERO's *body out upstage while* HECUBA *talks to the* VILLAGERS.

HECUBA. You fishermen work hard and build up your stocks. It'll be a lean winter.

TEMI. We can't! Our nets were torn on the bottom!

PORPOISE *(pointing to* HEROS's *body).* He promised us new nets!

NESTOR. Not one penny! That I refuse! (*He sneezes. Rubs his hands.*) Brr. I'll go and warm my hands by his fire.

A distant roll of thunder.

HECUBA. You women will have to work hard to make new ones. Start while it's light.

The VILLAGERS *hurry away and* NESTOR *hurries after the bier.*

NINE

Next morning.
Calm and clear. ISMENE *stands by the hut and watches* FISHERMEN *bring* HECUBA's *body up from the beach on a wooden trestle covered with sailcloth. The* MAN *walks ahead. The* FISHERMEN *stop but hold the trestle while they speak.*

MAN *(to* ISMENE*).* We found Hecuba's body on the beach.

TEMI *(to* MAN*).* We told the Greeks the storm blew itself out last night.

ORVO. They're shipping anchor fast so they catch the lull.

TEMI. We had a meeting. The old people wanted to send you off with the Greeks. But the young men came – they're not part of the meeting, they pushed in – and spoke against it. The Greeks are everywhere. We could all end up in the mines. We may have to take to the sea for a time. We'll burn her on the quay.

The FISHERMEN *take* HECUBA *out.* ISMENE *and the* MAN *are alone.*

ISMENE. The old Greek caught a fever last night. They say he shivered so hard the ship creaked. They're going fast – to see if they can get him home to die in Greece. Where did you find her?

MAN. The waterspout picked her up from the beach and carried her into the fields. She was caught in a fence like a piece of sheep's wool. When the spout passed over her it ripped out her hair and her eyes. Her tits were sticking up like knives. Her face was screwed up and her tongue – a long thin tongue – was poking out.

ISMENE. Since you've loved me my mind's begun to clear. Even yesterday I was calm.

MAN. I may disgust you.

ISMENE. No, never.

Off, one distant shout of the young men's voices.

ISMENE. What is that?

MAN. The funeral games. The young men starting the race. They have to be quick, to go out in the boats.

Poems, Stories and Essays for *The Woman*

HISTORY

The architect knows that a roof is supported by the building's foundations. Gilding the steeple doesn't strengthen foundations. Putting turrets and steeples on the roof will not make the building safer.

We know that our bodies, also, are subject to the physical laws of nature. We cannot *will* to have twenty fingers or jump twenty feet. Yet we think we can run our societies on such chicanery.

Because we have will and consciousness we think we can handle human affairs in a different way. This is as much as to say that if we *wish* the roof to be firm or are dazzled by the steeple in the sky then the building will hold together as if spellbound. Clearly our understanding of history is still only an alchemy and we live on philosopher's gold.

Societies, too, are subject to physical laws of nature. History teaches a truth that cannot be opposed by *will* any more than a madman who thinks he's Napoleon could conquer Europe. Yet in society whole classes make similar mistakes about their identity.

Why are our days crumbling and our times violent? Because we gild steeples. But in history truth – like the physical laws of nature – comes from the foundations. True culture is created there, not at the top.

I wish I could show some of you how to understand this. But some of you build your steeples high till their tops are lost in the clouds. Perhaps now you have nothing to do but fall. If so, take comfort in this: your debris will then join the foundations.

A STORY

In the mine there was a rumour that the mine owner had built himself a white palace next to the sun. This caused great confusion to the miners. They could imagine what a palace looked like. It would be like the holes they cut in the rock. But the holes would be bigger and even longer. (It was said that a man might stand upright in some of them.) But what was sun? And what was white? The miners had never seen white. Nor had their families who lived at the bottom of the shaft below the mine owner who lived near the top.

And one day a young miner decided to go to see the palace and come back to the miners and tell them what sort of thing white was. After his shift he started to climb up the shaft. It was a hard climb. Whenever he tired he slept in a crack in the side of the shaft. Sometimes there was a low roaring below him as a cage loaded with ore came up. At such times he hid in the side. At other times he heard a gentle sighing above him as an empty cage came down. Then he had to move very quickly to reach a hole. His shoulders and elbows were scraped raw by descending cages because he couldn't move quickly enough.

No one searched for him. In the weeks before he left he had hollowed out the roof of his tunnel. On the last day he had knocked it down. The charge hands had assumed he was buried under the fall of rock. One of them had marked the fallen rock with a piece of iron. The piece of iron meant that other miners should not be sent into this tunnel. Charge hands were punished (deprivation of food or, in the case of joking with miners, demotion to the job of miner) if they lost miners through unnatural causes. Natural death in the mine was through routine work. Accidents were not only against nature but even against regulations.

After a few days of climbing, the miner realised he could drop on to one of the roaring cages going up and in this way be carried to the top. He thought about it for a time. Four cages passed him before he risked jumping on to the next.

At the top he found the mine owner. The mine owner was paying his six-monthly visit to the mine. The mine owner threw a rock at the miner. He knew what a miner looked like because his father had insisted he learn the job from the bottom and so he had once been shown a drawing of a miner.

For some reason the miner knew he must be the mine owner. He said, 'I have come to see your palace. And please sir what is white?'

The mine owner smiled. Here was a good fellow, he thought, and he remembered how his father had told him to think favourably of miners. 'Well . . .' he said, looking at the sooty miner. 'White? . . .' he mused for a moment and then smiled and pointed to his head. 'My face,' he said, 'is white.'

With a whoop of joy the miner reached out, cut it off and dropped it down the shaft to the miners.

It would be better for them if those who know what white is also knew what black is.

A DARK MAN

Deep below mountains and cities and forests
In darkness he dug
Ore to give brightness
  But for him only a whip

Centuries later the tunnels were higher
Instead of the whip he was paid
Pieces of silver
  (Judas paid Christ)

In time he works on the top
They try to delude him with myths
'He lives in a world too dark for his simple mind
But his master will lead him'
  Yes, you can be sure
  When he got to the top
  They'd use the daylight to blind him!

The past is full of their crimes
No one will live in peace
Till the last of their crimes
Are known and condemned
  That is the purpose of history
  And why it is called just

ASTYANAX

When the child is taken the women wail
And stare in terror at the sky

Soldiers go among them as if
Under their steel there was only
Iron and wood

And so as not to frighten the child
We began to rehearse with a cardboard box

The women who were to protect him
Could only hold him with tenderness
Or the box would be crushed

So the child is taken

  How can we change the world
  With tenderness?

IN PRAISE OF BAD TIMES

At the start of things the creator put two men into the world. To
one he gave a carrot and some string and a stick so that he could
ride on the other's back. The other carried him and spent his
days reaching for the carrot dangled before his face.

The man on his back was pleased at the secret understanding he had of their situation. He smiled as he rode through the world and said, 'What it is to have knowledge!'

But the man who rode on the other's back was greedy. (In fairness it should be said that hunger would have had the same effect: history is implacable.) And one night he ate the carrot. In the morning he climbed on to the other man's back as usual. He dangled the empty string before his face. The man did not move forward. Instead he looked up and down and then to the sides. He was looking for his carrot.

The man on his back became angry. He raised his stick and brought it down sharply on the side of the other man's leg. The man shot forward. The man on his back was pleased again. That day they travelled farther than they'd ever done before in one day. Later in the year he even discovered how he could loop the string through the other man's mouth and efficiently point him in the direction he wanted to take. This also meant he didn't have to shout so often.

It might seem that the condition of the man on the other's back was now much improved. This would be an illusion. It was the condition of the man who carried him that was improved. It is far better to know the real taste of the whip than hanker after the illusory taste of the carrot. Such a man may be said to be wise.

But there are other men who could learn from the donkey.

ON THE RED FLOOR COVERING

H. covered the great stage
With a red floor cloth
That looked like the tongue
In an open mouth

On it the actors move
To speak their truth

In the world the great
Also walk before us
On a red carpet

But what do they speak?

ANOTHER STORY

A man lost on a journey halted to ask a woman directions. She asked his destination. He told her. She knew it. She gave him directions. The directions were right.

The man followed them. Yet he did not reach his destination. When he was old he abandoned his journey and took refuge in a hostel. One afternoon he lay in his bed staring through the window and fingering his unshaven chin. Through the window he saw the woman. He shouted after her 'Why did you send me on the wrong way?'

She stopped, said she was sorry to see him in this state, that the directions she'd given him had been right, but that when she'd asked him where he was he must have lied. Naturally she had given him the right directions from the place where he'd said he was.

No one should set out on a journey till they know where they are starting. Indeed you may not know – perhaps *never* know – your destination: but you must know where you start. How else can you do anything or go anywhere?

It follows that hope is not faith in the future but knowledge of the past. This hope is not an idle fiction but the surest of facts. It is a promise kept even before it's made.

But for those who hope falsely ... well, their condition is hopeless.

POMPEI

People who lived on the slope
Went to market each day
Met on street corners
Saw death in the arena
And passed by the sluices that carried water to wash out the blood
Took pains to bring up their children
Bought houses and saved against age
While over the city the mountain smoked

It's said that in those days of imperial violence
Men lived in a dream
Learned how to live with danger
And energy gave way to frantic fever

How far is the missile site from your house?

A STAGE DIRECTION

I put between brackets
The direction *has plague*
For a play

Then I was asked by the make-up technician
To look at the book of skin diseases

If god told me of sin on the last day
I would open this book and show him creation

Those who complain of science
Suffer from a disease

We hope science
Will cure it

A WOMAN

On a mountain I saw in the distance
Leaping and twisting
And lifting her arms as if stumbling
Or reaching for branches
A woman

I came close to see this wonder of nature
She was a smiling serious woman
On her path were such fissures and cracks
That leaping made her journey a dance

Strange dancing that twists yet goes forwards!
But also the arrow
The emblem of straightness
Has for its head
A corner

BLACK ANIMAL

In the ancient world there were silver mines. Few miners escaped from them. Of those that did only very few survived. The others soon died. They were not used to living above ground. And anyway most of them were caught and killed. They were easily recognised. Their bodies were crippled from working narrow seams. Their skin was dark and pitted. People who found them and took them back to the mine were rewarded. If it came out that someone had seen an escaped miner and not reported it then he was made to kneel beside the miner and be killed with him. First the miner was killed. Then the sword – wet with the miner's blood – was used to kill the other man. Such was the law.

This is a story about a miner who escaped. He knew he had to get far away from the mine very quickly. If he were seen near it he would certainly be taken. He travelled by night. During the day he slept in a hole or a ditch. He ate wild fruit and stolen vegetables and eggs. He drank from streams and puddles.

During the day he slept deeply and didn't dream. He cursed himself because this was dangerous. It would be safer to sleep as lightly as an animal. Then he would be alert the moment there was a risk. But his exhaustion overcame him and there was nothing he could do about it.

One morning he was walking along a path between dark bushes. It was already light and the sun had begun to rise over the horizon. He was anxious. Usually he was under cover by this time. But today he was unlucky. There was no undergrowth and though the bushes were dark the light would filter through them when the sun was higher. There were no ditches or rocks. He started to run. Suddenly the path turned and he found himself out in the open just as if he had been shaken from a box. All the countryside in front of him had been cleared for fields. In the distance there was a small group of houses. Far away a dog yelped. Then there was silence. He felt his heart beating.

Suddenly a flash of light. He made a small noise in his throat. A quarter of a mile away two men stood watching him. The light flashed again. One of the men held a sickle. They were harvesting.

The three stood stock still and stared at each other. The miner wanted to run back to the bushes. Hide. Dig himself into the ground. But he knew he must do nothing to rouse more suspicion. He started to walk round the edge of the field. As the distance between him and the men grew his terror grew so that he wanted to shout. He could tell the men were talking about him to one another. Then the shorter man started to walk towards him. The miner pretended not to see him and went on round the field at the same pace. Out of the corner of his eye he saw the man begin to hurry. He shouted. The miner turned and saw he was a boy. He stopped. The boy came towards him and stopped some way off. The miner said 'What?'

The boy turned and pointed to the other man 'My father . . .'

The man in the distance called 'Hey!'

The boy beckoned the miner with a swing of his arm. He started to walk back to his father. The miner followed slowly. It seemed to take a long time. The gap where the path entered the hedge got smaller. The miner's heart was quieter now. His breath passed in and out of his nose with a little whisper. The man stared at him all the time. The boy hurried and the gap between him and the miner grew as if he was setting the miner free. He went on at his slow pace and tried to hide his limp a little. His dirty black hair fell across his face but he didn't brush it away.

The boy reached the man and stood with his back to the miner. He could see the man talking to him and pausing to let him reply. The boy turned to face him and stepped back and to the side of his father. The miner could see the man's face clearly. It was round and stupid. The eyes were shrewd. The mouth was as tense as the mouth of someone silently totting up figures. The sickle hung from his left hand in the shadow.

The miner stopped. He was close enough now for the man to speak to him. The man said nothing. He seemed to be waiting for the miner to come closer. The miner stayed still. The man sauntered a few paces towards him. The boy didn't move. The man smiled slightly and then nodded in greeting. The miner gave a little nod back, almost a flinch.

'Going far?'

The man smiled again. The miner saw how intently he watched him. The blade of the sickle curled in the shadow as the man changed his grip.

The miner said 'Lost'.

'Ah. Stay here a few days. My older boy's ill. Help me with the harvest.'

The miner nodded.

'Get that coat off your back.' He turned to his son. 'Run to the house. Fetch your brother's sickle. Hurry.'

The boy started to run towards the houses a mile or so away.

They were silent and blue in the thin mist. The miner was filled with despair as the boy ran farther and farther away. To end like this. . .!

'Is that water?'

The man stared at the miner and then nodded. The miner limped to the pitcher lying a few yards to the side. He picked it up and a large stone that weighed down a folded cloth. He threw the pitcher. The man easily side-stepped. As he did so the miner threw the stone. It struck the side of his head with a thud. The man yelled. The miner ran at him, jerked the sickle from his waving arm and struck him three times in the head, chest and stomach. He had to pull the end free. The man sat down and tried to turn away. The miner swung at his throat. The man fell sideways. The miner turned towards the boy. He was running to the village so fast he could not scream. The miner turned back to the hedge. The boy saw a small dark figure on the left. A woman going towards the houses. She carried a basket on her head. Her back was towards them. The boy changed his direction and ran towards her. This took him closer to the miner. The miner ran forward. For a moment he was running towards a point ahead of the boy. As he got nearer the boy passed the point and the miner running after him. The gap closed. The boy turned to look. He was trying to scream. He had so little breath the sound came out as a groan. The miner could see the dirty soles and the chicken bones of the ankles and the flailing elbows. His breath made an animal roar. He reached the boy and swung at his back with the sickle. He missed. The force of the blow turned him aside. The gap between him and the boy widened. He ran. The gap closed. His breath screamed. He hacked at the boy's hip. The boy staggered to the side. He screamed. The miner killed him.

The woman had turned. She had lifted the basket from her head and was crouching to lower it to the ground. She dropped it. She stood still with her hand to her mouth. She ran a few yards towards the houses, stopped, walked a few paces towards the dead boy and then turned and ran screaming towards the houses.

The miner lurched back to the hedge. He passed the dead man. Blood was smeared on the stubble and there was a dark puddle in the furrows. He ran into the bushes.

The woman reached the houses. Children and other women ran out to meet her. A boy was sent to fetch the men from the fields. Some of the women went out to the dead bodies. At first they were afraid to go too close to them. Then a middle-aged woman went to the boy and began to wail. Other women went to the dead man.

The woman sat against the wall of the house. A little circle of grannies stood round her. They rubbed her wrists and forced water between her teeth. She was still crying and shuddering when the men arrived. The head man sent some of the men to fetch the bodies. The woman told her story over and over again.

'An animal. A black animal. At first I thought it was a great bird with a broken wing. Trying to fly over the field and dragging its broken wing along the ground. But it was an animal. Black.' The woman couldn't say any more. She repeated over and over 'An animal. Black. Black.'

The men formed into a hunting party and set out. The miner ran along the path till it was dark. Then he hid under a fallen tree.

TORTURER'S LAMENT

It's a hard life on duty all hours
Patrolling barracks
Guarding the depot

If there's an exercise it's bound to be hot
Or it never stops raining
It's church parade on the day of rest
And as if fighting wasn't enough
They bounce you out of bed
For fire drill

My wife nags
The canteen girls promise a bit on the side
Then let you down
They can't cook either

The sergeant's a swine to his own
The snotty little puke of a second lieutenant
Is so pig-scared of his men
His hand shakes when he salutes

Then you hear on the news
The investigations have got to stop
They take away the one chance you get to relax
The one bright spot in the grind
Is it decent?

You go in that little room
Dark like the pictures
That's where the action is
A chance to be your own boss
Use your imagination
Watch someone else crawl for a change

Now they want to take that away!
I ask: Is it fair?
They've got no idea
Let them come out here and try this life for a change

POEMS FROM A NOTEBOOK FOR *THE WOMAN*

1.

Who is this mad woman beating with her fists against heaven
As if the sky were a door to be opened to her?
Who? Who? Who? cries the prophetess when they come for an
    answer!
I Hecuba!
Bloody Hecuba with the lion's maul
And the coat matted with male lion's blood!

2.

Kill the little boy
His unripe body has organs
For seed

And if barren
His hands could hold a sword

His eyes playing like water
Wild in the sunlight now
Would narrow with purpose

3.

The plague in the poor quarter
Has started to spread to the rich quarter

Save our city!

4.

The emperor in his new clothes
Is preceded by a flag pole
On which flutters
A piece of the same material

5.

They danced
Later the invader came
And they saw they'd stamped out
Their graves

6.

Not trees in fog
The wet grass and mists
Of the north

Burning brick and stone
Marble and shadow
Men swift as snakes
Bloodier than tigers
And each instant clearly photographed
Evidence for the victim's family

NOTES ON ACTING *THE WOMAN*

The stage design is very simple. A few simple objects and even
these are simplified. They are not stylized. For example, the
temple steps are not made out of glass cubes. We want the audience
to think about the Trojans and not the temple steps. So we make
the steps suggest reality. When you stylize you may escape from

reality into fantasy. Our production is real. It has its feet on the ground. It is not over-realistic (as some Chekhov productions are) for a particular reason: we want to tell a story or analyse the truth. We don't want to record things but to show the connection between things, to show how one thing leads to another, how things go wrong and how they could be made to go well.

An actor should use each scene to prepare for the next. We must not become bogged down in each scene, weighed down with emotion, trapped in too much detail. We must reach forward to the next scene. We should be like a parliamentary candidate touring his constituency before an election. In every speech and at every doorstep call he makes he must be clear and truthful. But the election day is coming and if he is to do well on that day he must move on to the next speech or call. This doesn't mean he must gabble. He needs a practised, skilful way of telling the truth. The play comes to a halt if we play each scene with the emotional urgency we would use to tell someone their house was on fire. Perhaps we should say that most of the emotion occurs between the scenes and that the scenes show the consequences of these emotions. You can make a distinction between a blow and the consequences of a blow. Very few blows should be struck in the play because when they are struck they should be a knockout. So most of the blows occur before the scenes. The scene itself is the reeling effect of the blow.

This is very simple. It is what happens in human affairs. Most of our lives are spent reacting to events. For example, people who were not born at the time are still reacting to the effects of the world wars. This doesn't mean that we are spectators. We are struggling in a current, not hesitating on the bank or arguing whether to jump in.

We could make a crude distinction between the plays of Chekhov and the sort of play I write – the 'story play' or the 'theatre of history'. Of course it is also bad taste to overact in Chekhov. But many of Chekhov's characters are on the side-lines. They exist between the important events of history and so they have very little else apart from their emotional life. *We* must be caught up in the events of history. But we must also be in control. We must analyse these events, not merely reproduce them.

If we try to act this play in a Chekhovian way we get bad Chekhovian acting because the play is always struggling against our performance. We have to release the play into its natural freedom. That means that each character in the play wants to tell us his story. He does not want to relive it.

Imagine you are in a waiting-room – perhaps at a surgery or a government office. There is someone who wants to tell you their story – why they need money, housing or attention. Their mind, their words, their gesture, their 'performance' will concentrate on their need rather than the cause or condition of their need. They will not indulge their descriptions because it would not help them to do so. Only a con or liar indulges himself in this way. The others want the facts to be clear – and then you will *know* how they suffered. They will often say 'You see?' or 'You understand?' or 'That is so, isn't it?'. Only the obsessive is so involved in his story that he re-lives it. But he is unable to analyse or say what his need is. People who surrender themselves to obsessions go to madhouses. Our acting must not be an obsession with the past. It is directed to the future.

We must give emotion its proper place. But we must not imagine that it is a revelation of the whole truth.

We are acting the play on a large stage. This large stage is well suited to the play. It creates opportunities which we should use. We can think of the play as a story. The actors then become the illustrations of the story as well as the speakers of the text. When you are on the stage you should have a graphic sense. Use your acting as illustration. The artist emphasises salient features. So must the actor. Don't let emotion dictate the gesture. Find the gesture through emotion in rehearsal. But then work on the gesture. Find what is significant in it and use this. Omit everything superfluous. When the Trojan priests gasp 'Sacrilege' it is confusing if at the same time they bang their rods. Either of these is effective and can be made more effective by study. Another example: Ismene's mindlessness: is a smile more effective than giggling, or could giggling be broken up in such a way that it underlines a smile? Find the gestures which sum up a moment or character and work on these.

We find that on the large stage the relation between language and emotion is very important. We no longer hug the emotions to ourselves. But can we control the language even further? Suppose we think of ourselves as figures in a silent film onto which we dub our voices. This would free our voices from the dictates of the body. More of our emotion would then be transferred to energy and precision. We would use ourselves and not be used by our emotions. Artists should not prostitute themselves to their emotions any more than they should indulge the audience's emotions. Instead we need energy to polish, release and discipline our acting. Energy occurs when an emotion is transformed into an idea.

Emotion by itself is not truth. But when emotion shapes and demands ideas and actions that express it, then it begins to tell the truth. Emotion, once it is experienced and located in rehearsals, has to be converted into energy.

We don't want the abstract energy of American musicals. In these energy has no goal and without the music (which takes the place of analysis) they are boring. Nor do we want the frenetic energy of method acting. This also is based on emotion and not energy.

In acting for television we refine and make our acting appropriate to the small scale. Oddly enough, in our large theatre we must also refine. We don't adopt the bombast of the old actors (which incidentally was probably not as hammy as we think: bad acting has always been bad acting and good acting has always had something good in it). Nor do we adopt the medical twitch of method acting. We are not swept by emotion (as in ham acting) or glued to the emotional base (as in method acting). Our acting does not recreate. It recollects. Its energy is intellectual. It makes the particular general and the general particular. It finds the law in the incidental. Thus it restores moral importance to human behaviour.

(*These are some rough notes made during rehearsals of the first production of* The Woman.)

HANDS

The Woman: Part One Scene Twelve

The hands tell this story

The hands of the bystanders are clean
They make curving gestures
When they threaten the enemy their fingers close
Like rodents' teeth

The hands of the poor when they enter the scene
Beg
As flat and open as empty plates

When they reach the steps and see their enemies
They are united by need and hunger
Their hands become fists
That rise in a chorus of gestures
They change into weapons
They menace and flail

At first the hands of the son hold high
The red sword
In the military rite at the temple
When he backs from the crowd to the top of the steps
One flat palm is raised to push them away
He turns to beseech the goddess
They clasp in pleading
He turns to the crowd
Two flat palms pushing against the air

The hands of the soldiers
Primeval creatures armoured in steel
A bystander touches her ear
The earring's still there!

The assassin holds the son with one hand
The other pushes the knife in his back
The son falls like meat off a butcher's hook
We see the assassin's hand holding the knife
He is still
Like the butcher he waits
Till the meat comes to rest on the scales

Now the son's hands are feeble and old
They wander like dying mice
Over the steps

The crowd roars: The goddess!
Their hands wave like branches and clothes
In a storm
A voice: To the Greeks!
The hands swing in one common direction
Then waving and pushing
With gestures of hate and rejoicing
They take their curse to the shore

THE APPLE

Look the apple
Born in a cold spring
Becomes gold

Yet there is the glory of men
And the beauty of women
Made ugly by class

So winter come!
That we may see summer
Before we are old

HEROS: NO REASON

A little meteor fell on the earth
Like a straw in the proverb
So that it dropped from its course
To the arms of another sun
And swung in the spheres of a new world

Beauty and silver-wealth
And power that sways states
Have no reason
They fail like snow in the sun

It is said Canute laughed at his court on the sand
But the Leader waits for the tide
He claims he can walk on water
When the lie is big the Leader believes it
He says: I am the voice of the people!
But the people speak to each other

Reason and truth are the force
That changes the world
The Leader is crouched in his dark corner
An imbecile child in rags
Playing with reason and lies
And the bones of his army

For weeks the sun shone on the snow
Then the snow melted
The leaves fall in winter
And later the tree

THE ORCHARD

Still night
Bright stars over the orchard
I must answer the questions
Knotted even in the grass

That half the world are poor
That children die as if they were born long ago
Not in our time

In summer when these trees bear fruit
The children will be dead

COLD SPRING

This April is cold
Leaves smaller than babies' fists
The starling sits in a hole
Like an old woman looking out of her door
Waiting for rain to go
Factories turn upside down in the streets
To gaze at the sky

Who would not love virtue
To help the weak
Comfort the old
And instruct youth in the books of wisdom?

Each man's hand holds the same within ounces
Each man's hand is a signpost
The finger pointing to hell or freedom
Each man's hands are the scales of justice
He is weighed in the balance

Hands that would hold must strike
Our feet are as weary as Atlas's hands
  You who love virtue
  Love this cold spring too

SCENES OF WAR AND FREEDOM: A SHORT ESSAY

War and peace are taken to be mutually exclusive. But perhaps what we call peace has really always been a part of war. I do not mean that peace has been a time when men trained and armed for war. Certainly this is true. But I mean something else.

Perhaps war and peace have been phases in one total form of behaviour, one total form of society. If this is so, war would have to be seen not as the breaking down of peace but as its culmination. And then it would be an illusion to talk of a war to end war since there could be no peace able to protect itself.

An irrational society such as ours is divided into classes. This institutionalizes injustice. Injustice is not a passive state but one of increasing conflict. Why?

Firstly, an irrational society justifies its irrationality with myths. It teaches distorted beliefs: that the world is a jungle, men are animals, some men are more animal than others, all men are born to sin or with the need to be violent, only the hard prosper, most men wish to be led, happily others are born to be their leaders, and all this is either chosen by god or ordained by evolution. As we are still ignorant of many other things important to our welfare even these distortions might not be all that serious. But they also distort each man's view of himself. No man can accept that he is irrational and inferior and then behave rationally. A man's view of himself becomes part of his behaviour. It licenses it.

Secondly, and even more seriously, men's intellectual cast of mind has emotional consequences. They are born with the biological expectation that they have a right to live. When a child reaches consciousness this expectation leads into the conviction that he has a right to his humanity. In politics this becomes the desire for justice. How else could human beings be born into the world? How could evolution produce a consciousness of inferiority, an individual's natural conviction that he deserved to be punished, humiliated or deprived? A foetus burdened with this innate knowledge would shrivel in the womb. And if a man is taught these things, if society destroys his sense of dignity – and it is a matter of common fact that it very often does – then this social evaluation conflicts with an innate value. The emotional conflicts that follow, the way in which our need to love others is turned into a hatred of ourselves and others – these are the subjects of a socialist psychology. I want to point out here that these conflicts have political consequences. This is the way in which human character and judgement are distorted to produce fascism, crime, needless aggression, vandalism, social irresponsibility and the other evils which are said to be innate in man.

But there are other people who are told they have a natural superiority and a natural right to privilege and power. How can they have an innate conviction of this? Their reason cannot correspond with their emotion. Again emotional conflicts follow – with the same political consequences. These people act from fear. They are belligerent and reactionary. And their condition is exacerbated by the conflicts injustice produces in the other members of society.

One of the most degrading parts of this debasement of our species is racism. Racism is a human form of the behaviour of more primitive animals who, when they are humiliated or threatened, displace their anger and fear on those even more vulnerable than themselves. In the end injustice and intellectual distortion can so coarsen a society that its members despise out of indifference and kill out of boredom.

These are the ways in which men, who are not born to sin or with an innate need to be violent, become the makers of H-bombs and the organisers of death camps. In politics myths may invent reality.

A society both highly technological and irrational will inevitably lead to fascism and world war. An irrational society cannot devise a way to end war any more than a madman can devise reason. If a society is irrational enough to make H-bombs it must be so irrational that only chance can prevent it from using them. To make prevention sure society would have to be radically changed. It would have to be made rational.

Some actions are so horrendous that there is no moral justification for them. Obvious instances of this are wanton cruelty, genocide and the destruction of the world. Yet of two men facing each other with drawn knives one may be acting badly and the other well. Men are unique in their ability to reason and their actions should not be judged good because of the goodness of their motive: 'I meant it for the best.' Their motive must be based on a rational understanding of the world. We have a moral obligation to understand. At least this is true when we act as citizens, teachers, fathers, mothers and other representatives of society – when our actions have political consequences. The rational interpretation and understanding of men, society and history is socialism. It is a philosophy that has a rational explanation of irrational human behaviour. It is a guide to the practical action of making society rational. This cannot be done without difficulty and setbacks. It is hard to change the world, to escape from the old irrationalism. But these difficulties and setbacks can be explained by socialism. It is a philosophy which gives meaning to all significant action.

In our present time of great change we should not tell people to reform themselves by finding their soul, or to satisfy their desire for reason with inner peace. This is not a dark age when men can peacefully retire to monasteries. It is an age of darkness and of encroaching light. To retreat into inner peace in a world that makes H-bombs is a sign of despair. It is decadent to teach or counsel such a thing.

War and peace are the products of irrational society. They are siamese twins trying to strangle one another. There has to be a new conflict between war and freedom. This is the struggle for socialism. It will be won when society relates men to the world and each other in a rational way, a way without the distortions I have described.

It will be said that this is utopian. No. It is not a *wish*, it is derived from a rational analysis of our situation. Human nature, in its important aspects, is made by society. Our species makes itself through work and culture. We are not born good or evil but with the potential to be either. What we become is largely the consequence of our society and our experience in it. H-bombs and death camps cannot be blamed on human nature. They are the consequences of social organisation. It follows that war is not a consequence of human nature but of society. So a society without war is possible.

Such a society would be rational and have achieved freedom. The alternative is not an irrational society. Our species can no longer live with the irrational. Technology closes some of the doors of history as it opens others. The alternative is the destruction of earth and the life on it. This is the most important argument for socialism – not that it provides work, food and care but that without it irrationalism will bear its final fruit: the destruction of our species. Capitalism cannot avoid this catastrophe.

Perhaps the world will always be a place of some difficulty and often of hardship and loss. This does not mean that it will destroy us or that we must destroy it and ourselves. Freedom is possible.

THE TABLE

The four windows of this stone house face west
My long table stands before the one in the living room
On it are books of plays and poems
A dictionary and a guide to birds
Envelopes and carbons
A bowl of white narcissi
And a bowl of crocuses not yet open
What colour will they be?

The notebook bound in leather
From which this sheet was taken
Looks as solemn as a bible
But the metal clasps in the spine are open
And the sheets can be used

And lately I have eaten at this table
Two times a day I clear a place for the plate
The glass and knife and fork
To eat among the books and see through the window
Birds foraging in the garden

The keys of my typewriter
The crumbs and plans for work ahead
Bring me peace

Soldiers before battle who sit on the grass outside their tents
With fragments of food on their knife
May well feel this

FREE MAN
(For Paul)

In the ancient world there were silver mines. They were dug into the hillside or straight down in the ground. The tunnels were dark and narrow. They were lit by wicks floating in little jars of oil. The miners were men, women and children. They did not belong to families. They were black with filth. Their hair was matted. Their skin was calloused. They crouched and moved awkwardly. They looked like misshapen animals. Animals have grace. Even when they're dying – unless they fall into hunters' hands – their bodies often have dignity. But the miners were neither animals nor humans. They seem to have been invented by madmen. Overseers terrorized them with whips and sticks. The owner owned not only the miners and the mines but also the world above. Miners were not allowed to go into that world till they were dead. Then they were taken up and burned.

Once three young miners made a pact to run away. They'd make it look as if the roof of their tunnel had fallen in. No one would try to dig them out of the rubble. In time the tunnel would be cleared. But when their bones weren't found it would be too late to send out a hunting party.

They were expert at mining rock. They undermined the roof of their tunnel so that the roof held together and could be released with a few final blows. They also meant to save food. But they were not able to do this. And when they knocked the roof in it buried one of them. But the other two made their way to the bottom of the shaft. All the miners looked alike. No one questioned them. They hid in a hole below the shaft. They waited till a miner was tangled up in the wheels of a cart. In the brief commotion they got into the shaft and began to climb to the top.

Their bodies were contorted by crawling and were not useful for climbing. It took them three days to reach the top. When cages passed they hid in the fissures riddling the shaft walls. Far above they saw the little dot of light. They hadn't seen daylight before. If they'd gone straight into it it would have blinded them. But after three days they were already used to it. At the top they waited for night. Then they climbed out and ran away.

They slept in a wood. They stayed in the wood the next day. They ate berries and grass seeds. They sat in the bushes and talked. They had decided they must not stay together. If they went alone the chance that at least one of them would get away would be greater. They smiled at each other – but their lips grimaced with nervousness and fear. When it was dark one of the miners said 'Goodbye'. The other grunted. They left the wood in separate ways.

The miner knew he had to get as far from the mine as possible. Even in another country he would be in danger. His deformity would give him away. No miner was allowed to go free. Someone would take him prisoner and send him back to the mine. There would be a reward.

He walked at night and slept by day. He stole some of his food. The rest was wild. At first he thought about only a few things. How to get away, hide, eat. People were dangerous. He hid from them. But after some months he began to think of more things. First he noticed that the world was colder than the mine. Because he was tired he slept as soon as he lay down. But one night he woke up shivering. Next he found he need not be afraid of everyone. Some people ignored him. They looked up from the fields as he passed and then stooped back to their work. And perhaps only a few of them were happy. He saw hungry children crouching in dirt. They were too weak to play. Once a blind woman poked out her thin hand at him for alms. He saw pieces of men nailed to a gibbet. Another time he saw a group of men laughing and shouting orders in front of a house. They chased the family into the road. The son had to carry the old father in his arms as if he were the child. The men set fire to the house. The women sat on the ground and cried.

There was much beauty. The sky had as many expressions as a human face. Leaves were as restless as children's hands. The faces and bodies and gestures of women filled him with an unfathomable desire. He felt ugly when he watched them. But he tried to walk straighter and his feet felt lighter. At night he thought about the women he had seen that day. Then even the earth was good to lie against.

He was careful. He walked by day but hid when he saw anyone on a horse. He hurried past the big houses. He kept away from the roads and stayed on the paths. He knew that if he were taken back to the mine he'd be killed. Even if they put him back to work he'd soon die. He thought of his time in the mine as a grey corpse from which he'd crawled. Now his life had one purpose: not to go back. That was all. Everything else mattered very little to him. But at night he sometimes thought of the cruelty he'd seen in the world. People could not run away from that.

One day he came out of a wood. A girl ran towards him on a path across the field. A man with a stick chased her. He caught her and knocked her down. He beat her. The miner dropped back into the wood. Fortunately the man hadn't seen him. He hurried into the deepest part of the wood. He'd work his way round and come out beyond the path across the field. The wood was very thick. Thorns stuck into his arms and legs and sides. A swinging branch beat his back. His sweat brought mosquitoes. They stung his face. He heard the girl screaming. He turned and started to run back. He fought his way through the branches and undergrowth. Thorns tore his face. Suddenly he tasted blood. He lost his way. Then he was on the edge of the forest.

The girl lay across the path. From time to time her body jerked. The man crouched at the side of the field. He held his bowed head in his hands. He tore at his thick black hair. The stick was beside him where he'd thrown it on the path. Suddenly he stood up, took the stick and began to beat the girl. She screamed. The man struck her three times. His back was towards the miner. The miner came out of the wood and hurried towards him. He picked up a large stone. He was close to the man. The girl was on her back. She did not defend herself. Her body jerked. She made short gasping sounds like a madwoman. The man struck again, swinging his back, raising the stick high and bringing it down with the whole force of his body. The girl didn't react to the blow. Her body went on jerking in the same rhythm as before. She didn't scream as the stick struck her. Just went on gasping. Her open mouth was filled with a black shadow.

The man said 'You – you –'. He waved the stick in the air. The miner hit him on the head with the stone. He fell down across the girl. He didn't shout. He was unconscious. The woman opened her eyes. She was dazed and couldn't understand what had happened. She staggered to her feet. She looked at the man and then suddenly saw the miner. She stepped back, still gasping. She turned and ran away down the path. The miner watched her lurching and slipping. She fell down, crawled forward a little, got to her feet and looked back in panic. Then she ran on. The miner gasped noisily for breath. He looked at the man. His cheek was squashed against the path like the cheek of a sleeping child. His hand was open. The stick lay beside him. There was no blood.

The miner ran towards the wood. Suddenly he thought of the stick. He ran back, picked it up and ran into the forest. He hurried the rest of that day and all the night. For hours he said 'Fool. Fool. The risk!' at first aloud and then to himself. He ran to the rhythm of the words. It began to get light. He looked for a place to spend the day. The path crossed a wooded slope. He turned off and found a grassy dip. On one side a small boulder. He sat on it. The lush, thick grass was cool against his feet and ankles. He took the stopper from his water bottle and drank two big mouthfuls. He leant forward with his head bowed. He was tired but he did not fall asleep. He whispered to himself 'Fool. Fool. The danger!' He was bowed in thought for a long while, staring at his feet and the grass but not seeing them. 'Why?' he whispered. He let the question, spoken with his voice, sound in his head. 'Why?' His mind went back to the wood where he'd hidden with the miner. He remembered how they'd tried to smile at each other.

He thought of the man lying across the path. Perhaps the woman deserved to be beaten. No, she was in rags. Pale skin. Famished. He shrugged.

He slept half the day. Then he started to walk. For months he'd been able to walk faster. He still limped but he was not so crouched. Today he felt stronger, as if he'd learned something but didn't quite know what.

It was a mild day. Towards evening he stopped to watch a man unyoking his oxen. They walked wearily but quickly into their stall, looking for food.

During the next few weeks it became clearer to him. The mine was hell. But why had he run? It would have been easier to kill himself. He ran for the same reason that he'd helped the unknown girl. He learned why he was alive.

To take such risks! He laughed to himself. He would walk to a distant country. Perhaps cross the seas. In time he'd find work in a village and live in a house with friends. When he died they would bury him.

ODE

The world was old before it bore men
Its young passion was spent
Rocks were grey
Rivers had scoured the hills with wounds
And water healed them

The earth was not naked when we were born
Our cradle was green
Covered with bright flowers

We did not come as monsters half drowned in swamp
Or bone birds shrieking on windy shores
Our hands were already tools not weapons

Men were born to a wise old mother
Surely with such inheritance
We will love peace